WRITING YOUR LIFE

Patti Miller is a writer and teacher who lives in the Blue Mountains of New South Wales. Having taught general writing classes for ten years, Patti realised many people wanted to write their life story and designed workshops especially for them. This book grew out of those workshops and brings to a wide audience the techniques and skills which have inspired Patti's students.

WRITING YOUR LIFE

A journey of discovery

Patti Miller

ALLEN & UNWIN

for Dolly

© Patti Miller 1994

First published in 1994 by
Allen & Unwin
9 Atchison Street
St Leonards NSW 2065 Australia
Phone: (61 2) 9901 4088
Fax: (61 2) 9906 2218
E-mail: frontdesk@allen-unwin.com.au
URL: http://www.allen-unwin.com.au

National Library of Australia
Cataloguing-in-Publication entry:

Miller, Patti.
   Writing your life: a journey of discovery.

   ISBN 1 86373 641 7.

   1. Autobiography—Authorship.
   2. Creative writing. I. Title.

808.06692

Set in 11/13 Bembo by DOCUPRO, Sydney
Printed by Australian Print Group, Maryborough, Victoria

10 9 8 7 6 5

Contents

Acknowledgments

THE AUTHOR AND publishers are grateful to the following for permission to reproduce copyright material.

Russell Baker for extract from 'Life With Mother' by Russell Baker in *Inventing The Truth*, ed. William Zinsser, published by Houghton Mifflin Co.; Curtis Brown (Aust.) Pty Ltd for extract from *Tell Us About the Turkey Joe* by Alan Marshall; Gabrielle Dalton and Mayse Young for extract from *No Place for a Woman* by Gabrielle Dalton and Mayse Young, published by Pan Macmillan; Faber & Faber Ltd for extract from *The Watcher on the Cast-Iron Balcony* by Hal Porter; Fremantle Arts Centre Press for extract from *My Place* by Sally Morgan; McPhee Gribble Publishers for extract from *Poppy* by Drusilla Modjeska; Penguin Books Australia Ltd for extract from *A Fortunate Life* by Albert Facey; Alfred A. Knopf, Inc. for extract from *The Road From Coorain* by Jill Ker Conway; Random House UK Ltd for extract from *A House Among the Trees* by Joan Colebrook, published by Chatto &

Windus; Reed Books for extract from *Moon and Rainbow: The Autobiography of an Aboriginal* by Dick Roughsey.

Preface

THIS BOOK EXPLORES the adventure of writing your life story. A life story is the same as an autobiography, but I prefer 'life story' because, to me, it is a more informal and inviting term.

Writing Your Life came out of a series of writing workshops I first conducted at Varuna, the Eleanor Dark Writers' Centre at Katoomba in the Blue Mountains of New South Wales. The workshops were called Life Stories and were designed specifically for anyone who wanted to write the story of their life or the life story of a family member.

From the beginning, I found working with people on their own life story exciting and rewarding. The extraordinary courage and strength in ordinary people's lives can be overwhelming. I now believe that there is no such thing as an 'ordinary' life. Each life is unique, and even the most 'ordinary' person has known the mystery and revelations of life in his or her individual way.

I want to thank all the people who have attended the Life Stories writing workshops at Varuna and elsewhere. Most of what I know about life stories I have learned from them. If anyone ever needs their faith in the courage and infinite possibilities of humanity restored, they need only listen to the life stories of ordinary people. I want to thank my students for trusting me with the stories of their lives and for permitting me to use some of their writing in this book. To protect their privacy, I have not always used their real names.

I also want to thank the Eleanor Dark Foundation, especially Mick Dark, who donated Varuna to the people of Australia for use as a writers' centre, and Rhonda Flottmann, the former director of Varuna, who has supported and encouraged Life Stories from the beginning.

PART I
BEFORE YOU
START

1
The reasons why

Life is no brief candle for me. It is a sort of splendid torch which I have got hold of for the moment, and I want to make it burn as brightly as possible before handing it on to future generations.

George Bernard Shaw

EVERYONE CAN WRITE a life story. No matter what your achievements or disappointments, your life story is worth recording. You may not have been a general or a prime minister or a movie star, but you have lived and are living your own unique life. If you have dreamed by childhood creeks, played in a dusty schoolyard, kissed in the back row at the pictures, watched the sun rise after a partner has died, or lived through any of life's twists and turns, then you have a life story to write.

Although this book is about writing, it cannot avoid being also about the psychological and spiritual journey of 'writing the self'. The journey is one of discovery, and so this book is a kind of map of the terrain, indicating interesting paths to take and warning of difficult mountain ranges you might come to on your journey.

It doesn't matter whether you have done anything extraordinary in your life or not. Writing is first of all observation and then putting the observation into words. So it is how you see your life that matters. And despite having all the material on hand, writing the self can be a mysterious business. Once you start writing you may find there has been more to your life than you thought.

'Why do you want to write your life story?' It sounds like a simple question, but the answers to it are not always obvious. I asked Damaris, a workshop member, why she wanted to write her life story. She was well-dressed and sophisticated, and I imagined she had a comfortable income.

'Well, I seem to have lost my way in life,' Damaris said, 'and I thought writing about what I have done might help me find it.'

It was not what I expected to hear. A comfortable income is no safeguard against losing your way, but it can hide the fact from others, and from yourself. What really intrigued me was that Damaris was around 75 years old. I had thought losing one's way was the special anguish of the young or of those facing midlife crises.

Damaris taught me, again, the unsuspected richness beneath the surface of each person's life. Hers is one of the many reasons why people decide to write what they have done and thought and felt. Asking 'why?' is necessary, not to start writing (writing itself needs more concrete questions than 'why?'), but to focus on the task ahead.

You may not be able to answer the question right away. In fact, you may not really know why you are writing your life story until you finish. You may just have a gut feeling that it has to be done, and the reasons emerge as you write. Unexpected discovery is one of the many joys of writing.

But just asking the question is productive. Drop it into your mind and let it lie there uncoiling. It will nudge all sorts of things to the surface to use when you are ready to start.

You don't have to have lost your way like Damaris to want to write your life story. Most people have a mixture of four main motives:

1   So my children and grandchildren will know about me and my life.
2   So I can make sense of a divorce/loss/adoption/journey/discovery—any experience that has changed me.
3   So future generations will know what life was like in my day—a life as social history.
4   To share with others what I have learned from living.

The first motive, to record for future generations, is the most common reason people undertake to write their life story. It is no wonder, because from the beginning of time the telling of lineage and history, of what has gone before, has been at the heart of civilisation. It is a fundamental human need to know our past, our roots.

The second motive is more usual among people midway through life, or who have undergone an overwhelming experience. It may be a birth or a death or a divorce or an intense insight. Because the experience disrupts all of one's previous stories, there can be feelings of unreality, of being disconnected. Writing about such an experience can be a powerful way of reconnecting, of weaving all the pieces of your life back together.

The third motive is linked to the desire to know our history, which, in Australia, is a mixture of many histories. You have probably wished at some time that you knew what your grandparents' or even your parents' lives were really like. What was Australia like then? What was their reason for leaving their home country and coming to Australia? This is your chance to answer your descendants' questions.

The fourth motive is often mixed in with the other three. Nearly everyone wants to share something of what they have learned from living. It is part of the human personality to want to share insight and knowledge. We would all have to start from the beginning of civilisation every lifetime if others had not shared their thoughts with us.

Looked at together, the four main motives all come down to giving a history of the self, to validating a life. When looked at more closely, these categories splinter into as many stories as there are people, each of them unique.

INDIVIDUAL REASONS

Erica, 30, grew up in South Africa in a white family with a black nanny. It was as if she had two mothers, both of whom she loved. When Erica was 15, her nanny left her family's employ and Erica has not seen her since.

She wanted to write about this experience to try to come to terms with the loss of her black 'mother'.

Rosemary, 49, was a pharmacist. She had spent nine years in an Australian ashram and she wanted to share her personal journey towards self-knowledge.

Wilson, 48, came from a remote highland village in the Philippines. He wanted to write of his transition from a traditional village to the modern world of Australia. His story was to represent a whole people's experience of rapid social change.

Graeme, in his late 70s, liked to tell a good yarn about his long and interesting life. He wanted to write about his youth in a country town before the advent of wireless, television or the car.

These are some of the reasons of 'ordinary' people, although the more I work with people writing their life story, the more I realise that there is no such category as 'ordinary'. Every life, happy or tragic, famous or unknown, is extraordinary in its own way. I don't even agree with Tolstoy that all happy families are alike. Happiness is more difficult to write about because the processes of growth and renewal are less dramatic than those of destruction, but happiness is as unique as grief. There is continual wonder in the variety of human experience and motivation and I am often awed by the courage and passionate dedication of 'ordinary' people's lives.

The motive for writing your life story is the coiled spring beneath your writing. It will generate the energy to get you started and it can keep you going when it seems as though the story will never be finished.

Think about why you want to write your life story. Write

your motives as clearly as you can on a piece of paper and put the paper above your work table.

OUR STORIES: PERSONAL MYTHS

Children love to hear stories of their own escapades long before they can properly tell them themselves. In 'Tell Us About the Turkey, Joe', a favourite story of mine by Alan Marshall, a little boy listens to tales about his life told by his older brother: 'He looked at his brother expectantly and, as the brother spoke, the little boy's eyes shone, his lips parted, as one who listens to a thrilling story.' The brother then tells a number of stories about the boy narrowly avoiding disaster, such as when he was kicked by a cow and when a ladder fell on him. When he runs out of stories, 'The little boy stood in front of his brother, entreating him with his eyes. "What else was I in, Joe?" he pleaded.'

There are many stories of childhood adventures in every family. One of my mother's favourites is about herself and my sister, Kath. She has told it a hundred times. It is one of our family myths:

Dad went into town and Kath and I were the only ones out on the farm. I heard what sounded like footsteps on the roof. I went outside and there was Kath, two years old and her golden curls flying, running happily up and down on the roof—ten feet over my head. My heart nearly stopped. I ran around the side of the house to where the ladder was still leaning against the wall. I was eight months pregnant with Peter but I flew up there like an angel. Kath was just heading towards the edge with her unsteady two-year-old run and I just managed to grab her as she tripped. But when I got back to the top of the ladder it was impossible to climb back down with my huge belly and holding Kath. I couldn't get down. It was freezing cold on that tin roof and we sat there for three hours waiting for Dad to come home. You imagine sitting on a roof with a two-year-old for that long. I think Dad thought he had a mad wife when he came home and found Kath and me, eight months pregnant, sitting on the roof in the middle of winter.

The family always laughs when my mother tells this story. It is told and retold, not because the events are especially important in themselves but because it shows us what kind of person our mother is: that she is original and humorous; that she is someone whose life is not predictable and who has a wry sense of the ridiculous. It conveys an attitude of humour in the face of difficult situations which is part of her personal philosophy of life.

Why do we have such a desire to recount our lives? For both my mother and the little boy in Marshall's story, the recounting provides a kind of mirror of who they are. The stories tell them what kind of people they are, how they *imagine* themselves. If we cannot imagine ourselves, we cannot exist. If we have no image of ourselves, no picture of ourselves in our mind, we do not exist as a self. *Our stories create us.*

Our stories tell us and others what is significant and valuable about us. Our stories validate who we are; they are our personal myths.

Myth, in the sense in which I am using it, does not mean untruth. In fact, it means the opposite. Myths are the stories which convey the truths and values of a culture. Personal stories are repeated to convey truths and values about ourselves and so are mythical in their purpose. Myths give meaning to the events of nature and the connections between human beings and the world. If a people's myths are destroyed, its culture is also destroyed. The work of myth-makers or storytellers helps maintain a community's sense of meaning.

In our personal storytelling it is the meaning of our own lives that is being maintained. We seem to have a fundamental need to shape in some way the overwhelming mystery of living. The lack, in the West, of communally accepted myths about the meaning of life makes personal storytelling, or the mythologising of our lives, all the more necessary.

Your story will be worth writing, not for the quality of your life, but for the quality of your observation of it.

This is true of all writing, but especially of life stories. You need not have done anything spectacular to write an interesting story. Daily life, well observed, has all the ups and downs of a good story. Observing your life and the world around you is the starting point of all writing.

EGOTISTICAL?

Perhaps you are concerned that writing about the self is pandering to a desire of the ego. Don't worry, it is! Ego, or a sense of self, is a condition of our lives as human beings. Writing your life story will strengthen your sense of self.

Some say the self is an illusion. Eastern philosophies have held since ancient times that we create the illusion of self to convince ourselves that we exist. Recently, in an ABC radio program 'Writing the Self', the presenter, Simon Pitch, suggested that the self is 'a fiction that we create in order that we may exist'. Creating your self through writing your life story is, in that case, an attempt to prove that you exist. Still, if you are not yet ready to spend your life meditating on zen *koans*, (non-stories of zen buddhism designed to liberate one from ego), you will find writing your life story an exhilarating and rewarding process. Even if you are ready for such a discipline, writing your life may help you develop detachment as you learn to see your life as a story.

When you have written your life and show it to others, their pleasure in what you have written will give you another reward. The life stories I have read show me time after time that each life is miraculous and unique, and that at the same time we share so much. A glimpse of what made life valuable to you is one of the greatest treasures you can offer others.

2
How to use this book

If writing is thinking and discovery and selection and order and meaning, it is also awe and reverence and mystery and magic.

Toni Morrison

A LIFE STORY is different from any other writing in that your Self cannot be avoided. In essays, mentioning yourself is discouraged; in fiction, you can disguise yourself in other characters. In a life story it is necessary to reveal (or is it create?) yourself as author and central character.

Each person's story is unique. We all share birth, life, and death, and there is much else we have in common, but we each experience these events in our own way. We cannot remember our birth and cannot know our death; life, then, is our subject. The life-story writer is nothing if not ambitious!

You already have all the material for your book inside you. This book is about how to get the material onto the page. It tells you how to write your story so that it will be exciting to write and interesting to read.

Because you already have the content of your life story, it may seem easy just to write it down. But then you think: where do I start? what do I put in and what do I leave out? how do I stitch it together? what can I do to make it more than just a list of events? And so you come to a stop before you even start.

This book will help you get started and keep going until you are finished. Except, of course, that the writing of a life story is never finished. There is always that last mysterious chapter which must remain unwritten.

Some of the things we'll explore in this writing journey are: structure; point of view; style; what sources to use; how to retrieve memories; how to write interesting detail; how to bring your writing to life; how to write dialogue; how to decide what to put in and what to leave out; and what to do with your story when you are finished.

These topics are arranged into ten workshop chapters. In these workshops I don't tell you what to write—you already know what you want to write—but I do give advice on how to write.

A practical guide—the workshop chapters

One of the joys of writing the self is the thrill of exploration and discovery. For that reason I don't want to give a list of the steps to take, or the topics to write about (although there is a list of topics in Workshop x). Rather, these workshops will point you in the right direction, help you when you are lost, encourage you to keep going, warn of dangers, and point out places of interest you may not have thought of exploring.

Use each of the workshop chapters, then, as a page of a map. Pore over it for a while, getting an idea of the geography and enjoying the place names that other travellers have written on it. Then, map in hand, take out your pen or typewriter or word processor and start plotting your course. The exercises are like tickets. Try each exercise and see where it takes you. Enjoy the journey.

For ease of use, each workshop chapter, except Workshop x, is divided into four sections.

First comes a *general discussion* of the topic in which ideas and anecdotes are offered for you to think about, argue with, and be inspired by.

Reading consists of short extracts from published life stories (or autobiographies) which illustrate the topics under discussion. Some of the extracts are by experienced writers, others are by people who had not written anything before they wrote their life story. Read the extracts to see how published writers handle the issues. They may inspire you to try something new.

Writing exercises is where you start writing. There are a number of exercises, four in each workshop, all tested in many workshop groups. Try them. You will find that some result in a page or two while others will trigger a whole chapter. Each person responds differently to each exercise. There are a variety in each chapter, and some may be used over and over again, generating a different response each time. Try them one by one and see which ones work for you.

Life Story writers illustrates how the exercises work. I

have selected one or two responses to the exercises written by workshop members. These are short, many of them written in ten minutes. Read them to share in, and be inspired by, the lives and writing of 'ordinary' people.

You can work your way through the whole of *Writing Your Life,* starting at the first workshop and reading and writing your way to the end. Or, if you like, you can use random workshop chapters as the interest takes you. They have been organised for the most part around writing issues rather than life issues, and writing issues will come up at different times for different people. That being so, I have still tried to organise the topics in the order in which most people want to explore them. The chapters can be used one after the other or individually, so feel free to use the approach that suits you best.

Doing every exercise in the book will give you a large amount of material for your life story. You will, perhaps, produce all the material you need. But your life story will still need to be organised. Workshop IV, on structure, will give you suggestions about how to organise your material. If you like to organise first, turn to Workshop IV before you start.

As for the continuing work of writing your entire life, to paraphrase a well-known piece of advice: *you can only write one page at a time.* You don't have to organise your whole life at once. You only have to write a little each day. If you wrote just a page a day, at the end of the year you would have 365 pages! Even half a page every evening would give you a good-sized manuscript. So make sure you have enough light, sit down and make yourself comfortable, and *start writing.*

15

3
Rewards and difficulties

But warm, eager life—to be rooted in life—to learn, to desire to know, to feel, to think, to act. That is what I want. And nothing less. That is what I must try for.

Katherine Mansfield

WRITING ABOUT YOUR own life is more challenging and revealing than most other activities. It may seem like an innocent and straightforward task, but once you start you will soon discover that there is more to you and your story than you suspected. Many emotions lie hidden until you start writing. Many thoughts are focused through the act of writing.

The joys and the problems are often unexpected. There have been both tears and laughter in the Life Stories workshops as people have been surprised by their own lives. As you set out on your life story you will come across at least some of the rewards and difficulties.

16

THE REWARDS

This is my favourite story about the rewards of life-story writing.

After several workshops, Rebecca showed the first draft of her life story to her estranged husband—with some trepidation. She wanted him to know about her experience of the long and terrible nervous collapse which had eventually led to the break-up of their marriage. She expected him to be extremely angry and accusing because he had seen the events, and his part in them, in an entirely different way. A few months later I received a phone call from Rebecca. She told me with delight that she and Mark had reunited. They had always loved each other, and writing her life story had helped both of them remember the joy they had shared and sort through their pain so they were free to start again.

Of course, I'm not claiming that writing your life story will mend a broken marriage! Writing is joy and wonder and one of the best reasons I know of to get up in the morning, but I cannot claim that it is a cure-all for ailing relationships.

Still, Rebecca's story illustrates some of the very real rewards of exploring your life through the written word: the growth in self-knowledge and understanding; the sorting through of problems; the possibility of forgiveness and the freedom to make a new start; the joy of realising unknown strengths; the pleasure of reliving good times; and the value of sharing your experiences with others, including others in the future.

Self-knowledge

Growth in self-knowledge and understanding can come

about simply through presenting your life in words. It seems to be a similar process to psychoanalysis, except that in analysis you are telling your life, whereas here you are writing it. There is more shaping, more art if you will, to writing than in the free flow of analysis, but you can come to much of the same knowledge about yourself. This happens especially when you are writing about your childhood. New light can be shed on the present when you explore the past. Because writing about ourselves involves writing about those close to us (none of us has existed entirely in isolation), we can also gain understanding of those who may have hurt us. Problems or confusion can often be sorted through with the help of this new understanding.

Many people who have written about childhood trauma have found it has helped heal life-long hurts. Events which were inexplicable at the time can be re-evaluated through adult knowledge and experience via the concentrated creative process of writing. Writing cannot change neglect or abuse, but it offers insight into how and why, and the child's terrified incomprehension can at least be cleared away. Forgiveness does not necessarily follow, but when it does it can be the purest freedom.

Letting go

The freedom of letting go of old mistakes and hurts can be one of the greatest rewards of writing the self. The English poet Robert Graves called his first autobiography *Goodbye to All That,* and said that one of the main reasons he wrote it was to be free of his past, especially the trauma of war. He wanted to 'say goodbye to all that', to let go of the confusion and make a fresh start. Again, writing your life is not a remedy for all hurts, but there are healing rewards in the process of sorting through and writing what you know of yourself. The healing that comes from forgiving yourself or others can bring great freedom and the energy to begin again. The old saying 'It's never too late' is especially appropriate to writing your own life story.

Discovering strengths

The joy of realising unknown strengths is often an unexpected reward of recording your history. You may have intended simply to make a record for your children, but you find a whole new process happening. The setting down of trials and achievements can reveal strength and courage that have been quietly there all along. I particularly remember Carole, a throaty-voiced blonde with a low opinion of her abilities. When she started reading her life story to the group, her listeners were full of admiration for her courage in the face of tragedy, especially after the loss of her only son when he was barely nineteen. She began to see that she had more to offer others than she had ever realised.

Remembering happiness

There is also the pleasure of reliving forgotten happy events. You can become so immersed in present concerns that you don't recall for years the childhood day when you daringly rowed across the Parramatta River; the morning circus elephants drank at your dam; or the sunny afternoon you spent with your first love on a bushwalk in the Adelaide Hills.

Many people have exclaimed to me that they hadn't

thought of a particular event for 40 years or more and they are thrilled to rediscover it. It is like finding a treasured photograph or book that you had thought long gone.

Sharing

A reward that comes when you take the plunge and show your life story to a workshop group or to family and friends is the pleasure of sharing. Your children will take special pleasure in knowing more of your early life, especially as they get older themselves. Don't expect your teenagers to be wildly interested in your childhood, though—they are too busy making their own stories happen.

Friends will appreciate the trust you show in sharing your story with them. They may tell you that they have known some of the same trials and delighted in similar experiences and achievements. Your story may inspire them to begin writing their own.

In workshops, I have found that sharing a life story is possibly the most rewarding part of the process. A rare trust and warmth are generated when you offer the story of your life to another. In a sense you are entrusting them with your self, and I have invariably found the trust rewarded, even in groups of people who have never previously met each other. There are sometimes tears, sometimes laughter, often murmurs of recognition as each person reads their work aloud. There is wonder in the difference of our lives and, at the same time, joy in knowing that we are so much alike.

Creativity

One reward shared by everyone writing their life is the joy of creativity itself. How can writing your own life story be creative? Your life is a given; what place is there for creativity when you must be truthful? Look closely at the words 'life story'. Life is made of flesh and blood and breath, and stories are made of words. Translating a life into words is one of the most creative acts you can engage in—a virtual act of magic. The pleasure of creating your life in words is a magician's pleasure. Write, and enjoy all its rewards.

THE DIFFICULTIES

The difficulties of writing your life story must be faced. There are only a few real difficulties, but they often involve other people and so you must be ready to discuss them. The main problems are: the privacy of other people involved in your life; the unreliability of memory; and, most difficult of all, the pain of stirring up old emotions.

Other people's feelings

Paradoxically, the most pleasurable reward—sharing your life story with others—can also be the source of your most awkward problem. You cannot write about yourself without including something about your family and, quite simply, they may not like it.

Even if you filter what you write about them through rose-coloured glasses, they may still object. Some people do not like being written about. They feel that their privacy has been invaded and can be suspicious of your quite innocent motives. I suggest that you talk to them about the value and importance of writing and sharing your life story. Hopefully they will feel less threatened and be pleased that something of their life is also being recorded.

It is much more difficult if you have written about others without wearing rose-coloured glasses. Without the sweet pinkish hue your writing will be more honest, but be ready for disagreement. You may find that everyone disputes your version of events. One man came to a Life Stories workshop because he disagreed with his brother's account of their family and wanted to write his own version.

Weigh up your own motives and reconsider what you have written, and if you don't have all the information or if it offends to no purpose, you may find it necessary to edit. But sometimes a hard truth has to be told. If your family disagrees with your story but you believe it has to be written, tell them, 'This is the way I saw it. Feel free to write your own version.' It sounds tough, and it is. Holding on to your own truth is not always easy.

If what you write about others is both offensive and unsubstantiated and if it is published, the law may enter the picture. Several workshop members have been concerned about being sued over what they have written. Consider how important the issues are to you and if you still want to go ahead, talk to a lawyer.

I will discuss responsibility to others in more detail in the last chapter, because it is the most common concern of people writing about their life.

Unreliable memory

A more immediate problem is the fickle nature of your main source—memory. The old comment about memory playing tricks needs to be heeded. It can be difficult to remember which events happened and in what order. But there are ways of diving into memory and coming up with gold. Indeed, memory is such a crucial part of writing life stories that this book has a whole chapter on how to release its treasures.

Stirring up old emotions

An unavoidable difficulty, unless your life has been entirely free of unhappiness, is that painful episodes in the past will have to be faced again. To write effectively about events and emotions, you must, to a certain extent, relive them in your imagination. In one workshop, Shirley, now in her early 50s, found that writing about her childhood was too painful. She had seen her mother emotionally and physically abused by a violent husband, and as she tried to write about it, she found that her old emotions were still too strong to deal with. After talking it over with me, she decided not to continue writing about that period of her life.

Only you can decide whether you are ready to face the emotions the writing of your life may arouse. Many people find that writing about painful episodes is healing, but others may find that the time is not yet right, or that they would like further help before writing about those emotions.

Writing your life story is not quite like any other activity or hobby you may take up. It can be confronting; it is challenging and exciting. You are facing yourself as much as if you were sailing solo around the world, so it is a pursuit for the adventurous. Take care—and remember, the rewards make it more than worth the effort.

PART II
THE
WORKSHOP
CHAPTERS

4
Workshop I: Getting started

If a man will begin with certainties, he shall end in doubts, but if he will be content to begin with doubts, he shall end in certainties.

Sir Francis Bacon

GETTING STARTED IS always the most difficult part of any enterprise. With a life story, the beginning appears even more difficult. It seems impossible to know where to start or how to organise the whole conglomeration into some kind of order.

Do not be daunted. For a start, take the implication in Bacon's advice: be content to start with doubts. You do not have to be certain to begin anything. If we waited for certainty, most things would never be started. Starting anywhere is better than not starting at all. But there are simple ways of getting started that everyone can try. Because this is the beginning of your journey, I will detail some steps you can take to help you head in the right direction.

Remember, you can only take one step at a time. Concentrate on the step in front of you.

PREPARATION

For any journey, there are levels on which you must prepare: on the imaginative level by talking and reading about the places you are going to visit; and on the practical level by making lists, booking tickets, packing your bags and selecting your point of departure. Beginning to write your life story is similar. You need to prepare on different levels.

Read

Read through this book. To begin with, especially read the discussions that open each chapter. Read other life stories or autobiographies, but not too many at first, because they can be so fascinating that you could become an armchair traveller on the journey of life stories. One or two, however, will certainly give you itchy feet. Of course it's all right to continue reading them once you have begun to write, but do make sure you take a step along your own path first.

Talk

Talk with others about your project. Talking it over will give you more ideas and often lots of encouragement. Most people I talk to wish their father/mother/grandmother/great-uncle would write their life story. You will find more enthusiasm and excitement for your project than you may have expected. Also, once you have told a number of people you are going to do it, sooner or later you will have to start!

Collect

Assemble your material. I will elaborate on this in Chapter 5, but briefly, collect together your diaries, letters, records of any kind. Again, don't spend too much time on this as it is easy to use it as an excuse for not getting started. Dates and missing information can be added later if necessary.

Arrange

Arrange your work tools. If you can get hold of a word processor, it will save you months of time and also give you the chance to try different arrangements of your material. Otherwise, a loose-leaf notebook is useful because you can shift sections around easily. Many people, including myself, still use a pen and notebook for first drafts. It feels comfortable and relaxed and you can sit in an easy chair while you are doing it—a position that I find much more conducive to recalling memories! It is very useful also to have a noticeboard to which you can pin letters, photographs, notes, and scraps of scribbled memories.

Organise

Organise space for yourself. Albert Facey wrote *A Fortunate Life* on one end of the kitchen table while his wife peeled vegetables on the other, but most people need a separate space to work. It is a good idea to set up a table so that you can leave all your work materials in place without having to pick them up before every meal. On the other hand, some people work best with a notebook on their lap on the sofa, in the sunroom, or down the backyard under a tree. You know your own best work-

ing conditions: create them for yourself so that you have
no more excuses.

Find time

Finding time can be more difficult than making space.
Work, children, grandchildren, the house, community
projects, the garden, all are important. If you wait for a
spare hour or two you may never get started or finished.
Make a regular time and let other people know you are
working during that time so they don't call in for a cup
of tea just as you're starting. It doesn't have to be
long—half an hour each evening when everyone else is
in bed or two or three hours on the weekend will get
you a long way. It is important to establish a rhythm of
working, at least for those of us who are creatures of
habit. It makes settling down to write much easier.

Plan

You don't have to plan the whole book before you start
writing. You can simply start on the exercises and see
what develops as you go. Select a particular time or event
to begin with and the structure will emerge as you write.

If you want to make an outline or plan your structure
before you begin, see Workshop VI on structure and
also the list of topics in Workshop X.

Establish a writing ritual

If you find it difficult to be disciplined about your
writing, you may find it useful to have a ritual for
beginning. For example, I say, 'Now let's have a cup of
coffee and think of nothing for fifteen minutes, and then
I'm allowed to start writing'. A short ritual during which

you do not permit yourself to think about writing is a cunning way of making an undisciplined mind desperate to start. It doesn't have to be a coffee break: try anything you find soothing—walking about the garden, straightening all the books on the shelf, sitting in the sun with the cat. Then select your point of departure and let the journey of your life story begin.

It doesn't have to be perfect first time

Almost all writers rewrite. It is part of the process to write a first draft which may be rough, and to then work on it, refining the structure and style. First you pour out, then you edit. If you always try to get it right first time, your concern for the perfect word could block a new and rewarding idea from emerging. Don't worry if your expression is rough and clumsy at first. You can always go back and rewrite as you become more experienced.

WAYS TO BEGIN

Now that you are prepared, there are countless ways you can begin. The following are some possibilities to consider. They are not topics—I will suggest some topics in Workshop X—but a discussion of writing structures you can use to start with.

Fact

Start with a fact about yourself. This is a deceptively simple suggestion, for once you start considering the facts they multiply in all directions. A logical stepping-off point is the date, place and conditions of your birth. It may appear as a blunt statement as in Clive James's *Unreliable Memoirs,* which begins: 'I was born in 1939.'

James follows this with: 'The other big event of that year was the outbreak of the Second World War, but for the moment that did not affect me.' Suddenly, the bald fact has become a revelation of James's conscious self-cen-tredness and his comic style of juxtaposing unlikely events.

James has used the facts to reveal truths about himself. Remember that while facts are true, they are not nec-essarily truths. If you reveal some truth in your opening, it will be more effective. For example, try to see what there is in the date, place or conditions of your birth that may have influenced your life. Were you born during a war? Were you born in the country? Did you arrive early? Was there a flood that year? Which star sign were you born under? Were there brothers and sisters waiting for you? Who were your parents? What have your parents told you of your arrival? Who was the prime minister that year? The facts can expand in any direction.

There are endless other facts about yourself that would be just as effective as an opening. One of the most intriguing opening facts I have read is in *Watcher on the Cast-Iron Balcony,* by Hal Porter, which begins: 'In a half-century of living I have seen two corpses, two only.'

Anecdote

An anecdote, or yarn, is an engaging way to begin. This can be a characteristic story about you or your family background that tells something significant about you. Sally Morgan begins *My Place* with a story about visiting her father in hospital. We see as we read on that an ill and emotionally disturbed father was a powerful influence in her childhood. A story from your childhood that you or one of your parents has often told may be the perfect beginning.

An image

Often there are pictures in the mind that seem to hold special significance. It may be a scene, an incident, an expression on a face; for some reason the particular picture is etched on our minds. *Poppy,* by Drusilla Modjeska, begins with the image of an umbilical cord being cut. We immediately feel the separation between mother and child and as we read on we discover that this is one of the main themes of the book. Think about your life and see if there is some place you often think about: a house, a street, a figure on a hillside, a particular smile. Opening with an image can be a tantalising way to start. It lends a sense of mystery and the possibility of discovery.

A thought or observation

It is generally more interesting to start with something tangible—a fact, image or story—but an abstract idea can be a provocative opening. The New Zealand writer Frank Sargeson opens his autobiography, *Memoirs of a Peon*, with the comment, 'So here I am stung by the snake of memory'. He immediately has our attention because we can all relate to memories and how they take hold of us.

A philosophical observation as an opening carries the danger of being too weighty and portentous. A way of avoiding this is to make your abstract comment brief and let it lead into a story. If your life is one in which a

33

philosophical frame of mind has been important, it may be most appropriate to open with a thought or observation.

However or wherever you decide to start, your words are not set in concrete. You can always decide later to change the beginning. You may find a better one halfway through or at the end. Don't spend too much time worrying about where to begin. Again, it is better to start in any old place than not to start at all.

READING

My Place

The hospital again, and the echo of my reluctant feet through the long, empty corridors. I hated hospitals and hospital smells. I hated the bare boards that gleamed with newly applied polish, the dust-free window sills, and the flashes of shiny chrome that snatched my distorted shape as we hurried past. I was a grubby five-year-old in an alien environment.

Sometimes, I hated Dad for being sick and Mum for making me visit him. Mum only occasionally brought my younger sister and brother, Jill and Billy. I was always in the jockey's seat. My presence ensured no arguments. Mum was sick of arguments, sick and tired.

I sighed in anticipation as we reached the end of the final corridor. The Doors were waiting for me again. Big, chunky doors with thick glass insets in the top. They swung on heavy brass hinges, and when I pushed in, I imagined they were pushing out. If it weren't for Mum's added weight, which was considerable, I'd have gone sprawling every time.

The Doors were covered in green linoleum. The

linoleum had a swirl of white and the pattern reminded me of one of Mum's special rainbow cakes. She made them a cream colour with a swirl of pink and chocolate. I thought they were magic. There was no magic in The Doors, I knew what was behind them. Now and then, I would give an awkward jump and try to peer through the glass and into the ward. Even though I was tall for my age, I never quite made it. All I accomplished was bruises to my knobbly knees and smudged finger marks on the bottom of the glass.

Sometimes, I pretended Dad wasn't really sick. I'd imagine that I'd walk through The Doors and he'd be smiling at me. 'Of course I'm not sick,' he'd say. 'Come and sit on my lap and talk to me.' And Mum would be there, laughing, and all of us would be happy. That was why I used to leap up and try and look through the glass. I always hoped that, magically, the view would change.

Our entry into the ward never failed to be a major event. The men there had few visitors. We were as important as the Red Cross lady who came around selling lollies and magazines.

'Well, *look* who's here,' they called.

'I think she's gotten taller, what do ya reckon, Tom?'

'Fancy seeing you again, little girl.' I knew they weren't really surprised to see me; it was just a game they played.

After such an enthusiastic welcome, Mum would try and prompt me to talk. 'Say hello, darling,' she encouraged, as she gave me a quick dig in the back. My silences were embarrassing to Mum. She usually covered up for me by telling everyone I was shy. Actually, I was more scared than shy. I felt if I said anything at all I'd just fall apart. There'd be me, in pieces on the floor. I was full of secret fears.

The men on the ward didn't give up easily. They continued their banter in the hope of winning me over.

'Come on sweetie, come over here and talk to me,' one old man coaxed as he held out a Fantale toffee. My feet were glued to the floor. I couldn't have moved even if I'd wanted to. This man reminded me of a ghost. His close-cropped hair stood straight up, like short white strands of toothbrush nylon. His right leg was missing below the knee, and his loose skin reminded me of a plucked chicken. He tried to encourage me closer by leaning forward and holding out two Fantales. I waited for him to fall out of bed; I was sure he would if he leant any further.

I kept telling myself he wasn't really a ghost, just an Old Soldier. Mum had confided that all these men were Old Soldiers. She lowered her voice when she told me, as though it was important. She had a fondness for them I didn't understand. I often wondered why Old Soldiers were so special. All of these men were missing arms or legs. Dad was the only one who was all there.

I tried not to look directly at any of them; I knew it was rude to stare. Once, I sat puzzling over a pair of wooden crutches for ages and Mum had been annoyed. I was trying to imagine what it would be like being lop-sided. Could I get by with only one of my monkey arms or legs? That's what I called them. They weren't hairy but they were long and skinny and I didn't like them.

I found it hard to comprehend that you could have so many parts missing and still live.

In this opening chapter of *My Place*, by Sally Morgan (Fremantle Arts Centre Press, 1987) there is a combination of images and anecdote. On first reading, it is simply an account of a visit to her father in hospital when she was a child. It is interesting in itself and many readers would relate to the child's experience of having to visit a relative in hospital. But this anecdote is also full of images that give clues about her life story. The most powerful of these is the image of The Doors which she tries to see through to a better life. We soon realise that this image reflects her constant attempts to see through the heavy closed door of her past.

The comment, 'I found it hard to comprehend that you could have so many parts missing and still live' also hints at the feeling she has that many parts of her life are missing. As you read *My Place*, you will see how it develops into a search for those missing parts.

WRITING EXERCISES

1 First fact

What is the first thing you want known about yourself? Your date of birth? A character trait? Your appearance? Your ancestry? When your parents first met? A strongly held belief? A remarkable feat? Your moment of glory? It is up to you to decide on the kind of fact you want to start with. Write it down and see where it leads you. Let it expand. Many writing books say that to expand on a fact you should ask who? what? when? where? why? how? These questions can be useful but they can also be stiff and limiting. I prefer to let the mind free-associate— simply write the fact and see what floats up from your mind next. Rational questions will call up sensible answers, but it can be more exciting to follow the mysterious and often revealing associations of your mind.

37

2 Newspapers

Go to a library and find newspapers of the day and year you were born. Look at the local, national and international news. Take an item that catches your interest—it doesn't have to be headline news—and write about your birth in relation to it. You could also write about your birth in the context of a number of news items from that day.

3 Childhood

Think of a story from your early childhood that you have often told over the years. If you can't think of one, ask your family. They will be able to tell you one of your stories word for word. Write the story down and try to make it as sensory as possible. Describe the clothes people were wearing, the weather, the kind of furniture, the sound of people's voices, and so on.

4 Parents

Write a page about either or both of your parents. For each, write about a particular incident involving them rather than about their general characteristics. If you did not know your parents, write about two people who were important in your upbringing. What did they look like? Do you look like either one? What work did they do? What are your early memories of them? Try to connect aspects of them to yourself. Parents are so influential in almost everyone's life that they cannot be truthfully left out of a life story.

LIFE STORY WRITERS

The following piece, by Damaris F., is a response to the first exercise. You will notice how it moves from fact to description to anecdote. In a ten-minute exercise you don't have time to edit your thoughts and it can be surprising where you end up.

Percy

I was born 'almost a war baby', that is 1919, on a Friday the 13th with Cancer overhead and a full moon. We, being my mother, and my mother's mother, lived on the outskirts of North London, my father had died a few months after I was born. I don't really remember the house, only what I can imagine from old photographs, but when I was about four years old, we moved to a new house some miles away, but further in the country, and with us came Pete, a white bull terrier. He was not jealous when I was born and was my companion and guardian. I actually modelled him in putty on the door of the coal shed, and my 'masterpiece' remained there long after poor old Pete was dead.

Not very far from the house was an old farmstead, and every afternoon we would walk down the road carrying a large brown jug, and watch the cows being milked by a farm-hand, and then fill the jug with warm fresh milk. I loved the farm and the earthy smell of the animals, the cows, the gigantic working horses, clucky chickens, and the quacking ducks, and even the noisy geese which used to chase me, and the excitement of finding their eggs sometimes.

There was also a big white pig, and as pigs will do, she had a large litter with one runt, which I adopted and called Percy. I can't think where I found such a name . . . but anyway I would help to feed him with a baby's bottle, and play with him, and tell him long stories. Being an only child there was no one around my age I could tell my woes to, except Percy . . . Then one afternoon we went to the farm as usual, but I couldn't find Percy, who by now was a nice fat little piglet. The farmer and his wife looked the other way and disappeared into their house. Finally my mother told me we were going to have roast pork for Sunday dinner. The penny dropped, and I burst into uncontrollable tears, while my mother carried home one of Percy's legs . . . I didn't have any Sunday dinner. I went down to the bottom of the garden, and ate gooseberries instead. I still remember Percy.

This next piece, by Pamela C., is an extract from a response to the fourth exercise. Further on in Pamela's story, it becomes clear that much of her life has been a reaction against her father, so beginning with her feelings about him is especially appropriate.

Myself alone

The year is 1952; the setting Sydney. I am eighteen years old, and I hate my father.

I love my mother, despite the aura of martyrdom she dons like an old woman's winter shawl. It is her nature to comply, and in the role of peacemaker she does not even receive that honour due to the 'weaker vessel'. A strange household, where an unorthodox man born of orthodox Jews, applies his personally devised rules to himself and his family, yet quotes the Christian Bible.

Arriving at the age of perception to realise you are the daughter of an ultra chauvinist is the first emotional cold shower for a young girl.

I readily admit at social gatherings to being proud

of his ready wit and the ease with which he entertains his doting audiences. I am delighted on rare public occasions, when he invites me to dance. We move well together and I would wish for no other partner. My father's sense of rhythm and practised manipulation have made females long before me, and certainly since, believe they sway in the arms of Astaire.

Some say that we are alike but I reject this totally. He may well be a charmingly mannered, entertaining fellow at parties, but to his family, he is a selfish tyrant. Fellow workers at his office see only an impeccably dressed, agreeable man to whom they bring their problems for solution; their sins for absolution.

Mother and I are not permitted the frailty of occasional sin. Father cannot cope with emotion on a personal level. We cannot disagree with him, criticise, or thwart him. On race days we cannot even speak to him. He is a very superstitious gambler, and several years ago he accidentally kissed Mother goodbye as he left for Randwick racecourse. Whether that unusual physical contact resulted in the magic moment when a bookmaker thrust pound notes into Father's normally hollow hands is doubtful; but Mother is now kissed regularly every race day.

We have always lived at Coogee. We move from rented flat to rented flat, within a short radius of the beach. There was a time when Father took me to the beach on Sunday morning; Mother at home basting the roast and swatting fat flies from the tiny kitchen. As I was only five or six, I was not concerned when ladies in their brief swimsuits joined us on our beach towels. They chatted and laughed a lot, particularly when Father rubbed their backs with coconut oil, but as long as they didn't pat my head and say I was 'the spittin' image of him', I was content to fill my bucket and make sandcastles on his feet. I didn't tell Mother about it. The walk back always made me tired and it was an effort to eat, even when there was Yorkshire pudding. I think she knew anyway.

Turn to the next workshop for information on sources you can draw on as you continue with your life story.

5
Workshop II: Sources

Time present and time past
Are both perhaps present in time future
And time future contained in time past.

T.S. Eliot

ONE DAY WHEN you have finished your life story, and probably far in the future, others will read your manuscript or book and be moved by your life. Because of the intrinsic magic of words they will feel some of your delight, your sorrow and your wonder in existence. Your emotions and experiences will live again in their imaginations.

This sharing of another's existence is, I believe, the main reason we read life stories, but a life story is also a source of information. It is an account of a life and a way of life, and is therefore an historical source. It doesn't matter whether you have been the prime minister or the mayor or the owner of the corner shop; your life story will become a source of information about the past.

Most of our knowledge about the pioneering days in Australia comes from the journals and letters of ordinary settlers, such as *The Letters of Rachel Henning* (Penguin, 1969). Her letters to her family give a lively picture of life in nineteenth-century Australia. Perhaps your life story will become a valuable source of knowledge about life in the twentieth century.

This does not mean you should just record the facts. It simply means that you may want to expand your own sources so that you give a wider and more accurate picture of your life and times.

Every piece of writing is like a cloth woven of threads from other cloths. We cannot weave our life from thin air. The sources of the threads we weave are many and include: memory; library research; family interviews; journals, letters and photographs; public records; and specific agencies and organisations.

Memory

Memory is the storehouse of our lives, huge and crowded and often dark. Parts of it hardly ever see the light, and parts are perhaps best left forgotten. There are other parts, however, that we visit often, gazing at the individual memories stored there and handling them with tenderness so that they become softer and sweeter with each caress. But the polish of nostalgia adds a shine that may not be entirely truthful.

Memory is such an important source that it requires a chapter of its own. For the moment let me only acknowledge memory as the life-story writer's primary source.

Library research

Research is a fascinating way to check your memory and add to your story. Following up a lead through books and newspapers can be as thrilling as a treasure hunt. One piece of information leads to another, and like a detective you follow the clues and discover all kinds of treasures as you go.

You may use library research to answer a variety of specific questions. What was the name of that street where I used to ride my billycart? Who were those three children killed in the bushfire when I was seven? What year was it when the Harbour Bridge was begun and Dad found a job at last? Which battle in France must it have been in which Uncle Stan was killed at Christmas in 1916? How much did milk cost when I was a kid? Who was the prime minister when I was born? All these questions can be answered by research in the local or the state library. Look in books of local history, general history and social history, and in local and national newspapers. If your library does not hold back copies of the local newspaper, try the newspaper office or your state library. Your state library also holds original journals, which you may need a special reader's ticket to look at. I have always found that librarians are very helpful and will show you how to find the information you want.

Articles and even advertisements from newspapers of earlier periods in your life can be valuable reminders of the social climate of the time. In the NSW State Library, I came across an advertisement in a 1950s newspaper in which a vicar recommended a brand of cigarettes! I can't imagine any minister of religion these days publicly recommending smoking. Sometimes we forget how

45

much times have changed. The discovery of little details like this can jog memories of a whole period.

Some people may like to start at the library, checking facts and gathering information. If you prefer to gather all your material first, that's all right, that's your way of working. But I find a large body of disconnected information a daunting way to begin. I suggest you start writing first, gather your facts as you go, and weave in information where it is needed.

Family interviews

Interviews with family members are an important but often difficult source. Family members will often know more about a particular person or incident than you do, or at least another version of the story! Older brothers or sisters and aunts and uncles can be especially helpful in filling in details and providing anecdotes about your parents. The problem is that some people do not like being asked questions.

It is therefore best to make your 'interview' as relaxed as possible, preferably an informal chat. A loose, rambling conversation may produce more interesting information than a stiff question-and-answer interview. But don't try to hide the fact that you are 'fishing for information'. Most people will see that you are trying to get something out of them and will resist. If you tell them why you want to know, however, in most cases they will be happy to volunteer information.

If there is conflict or secrets in your family you may meet quite a lot of resistance. A workshop student, Gloria, told me of her interviews with her family as she looked for her father, who had left when she was a child.

It was very slow work finding out his background and what had happened to him, as everyone seemed to be hiding something. She eventually discovered as she widened her search that on his side of the family she had dozens of Aboriginal relatives whom she'd never met or even heard of.

With patient questions she eventually made contact with her father and arranged to meet him. Sadly, he died just a couple of weeks before they were able to meet.

But that wasn't the end of the story. Her newly discovered Aboriginal heritage had deepened her life story and added a richness she could not have imagined. Her advice to anyone trying to find out more about their own past was to be patient and persistent.

So make clear your intentions; reassure people that your aim is not to hurt or upset. Don't ask all your questions at once; take it slowly.

You may find that the people most reluctant to be questioned are your own parents. Sometimes this is because there has been trauma in their lives and, coming from a generation that believes it is best to 'leave things alone', they don't want to talk about it. Even when they have no painful memories they may be anxious about your motives. Once again, take it slowly, give them time, be reassuring, show them what you have already written. Involving others in the process of your writing is one of the best ways to overcome their doubts.

Some people may find it easier to answer your queries if you write out your questions and ask them to write their answers. This way they have time to think about their responses and the chance to express them in their own words.

Using a tape recorder is a practical way of keeping a record of a conversation, although many people find this threatening. Check whether your 'interviewee' is comfortable with the idea before you switch it on.

Listen for what is not said as well as what is said. Some silences say more than thousands of words.

Journals, letters and photographs

These are the tangible treasures of most people's lives. If you ask people what they would save in case of flood or fire, most will say 'the family photos'. Although these have no monetary value, they are often valued above expensive furniture, clothes, appliances. This is because photos, letters and journals are our evidence of having lived—without which most of us could not go on.

The fact that we need to prove, even to ourselves—first of all to ourselves—that we really exist, is intriguing. It's a central issue of philosophy, but here it is enough to say that keeping photos, mementos, letters, and journals is probably not foolish and sentimental but the result of a basic human need to 'keep the evidence'.

The 'evidence' can be used either directly or as a memory key. Putting letters or journal extracts directly into your story can make it more lively and lend immediacy to the times you are describing. The events are fresh and unexamined, not layered over with years of retelling or interpretation. Still, unless your writing in these records was very disciplined, direct extracts are best used sparingly and edited to keep only the best descriptions and insights.

Using letters and journals, photos and mementos as memory keys is also worth trying. Rereading journals and gazing at old photos is a good way to open the door to lost memories. You may not put the material directly into your story, but it can be a starting point or you can paraphrase the information. There is more about using this material as a way of opening the storehouse of memory in Workshop III. Take out your faded letters from old lovers and the journal you kept when you were sixteen. Find old school reports, trophies, ribbons and cards. Ask friends for the letters you wrote them when you travelled overseas. Pull out the diary you kept during the war; the embroidered hanky your daughter made for you; the poem you wrote when you were in hospital. These are the evidence of your life.

While we are on the topic of journals, I suggest you keep a journal while you are writing your life story. In it you can record your research findings and your problems and successes with the writing. This type of journal can have many uses. It can help keep you going when the writing is difficult, as it is a most sympathetic listener! It can also be fascinating to read through once you have finished your life story. You may realise that the writing of your life has been as much a journey as your life itself. Finally, a journal of your writing progress can help you structure your life story. See Workshop VI for ideas on how the process of discovery itself can be used as a way of tying all your different pieces together.

Public records

Public records are a useful source, especially for checking the 'facts' your memory supplies. They provide the official details, the curious bare bones of your existence.

On their own they don't say much, but they are the community's record of your life and their emotionless formality can stand in striking contrast to the actual rich texture of your living.

You can check dates, places and names against the records held by the government (especially the Registrar of Births, Deaths and Marriages), the church, the armed services, community organisations, public and private institutions, and schools. Call in at their offices or write to them with your list of questions. Appendix B at the back of this book has some addresses you could try. A fee is required in some cases, particularly with regard to government records.

Specific agencies and organisations

You will soon realise, as you research your own life, that you are not alone. All over Australia there are organisations for people wanting to find out about their backgrounds.

Look in the telephone book for historical societies and genealogical societies. Public libraries often have computer records and other facilities for those researching their family history. In writing your life story, you may want to include some family history to give a sense of where you have come from.

Adoption: For some people, their origin becomes an overriding concern because it has been lost or hidden through adoption. No matter how happy their adopted life has been, such people often have a special need to write their life story, perhaps as a way of filling in the unknowns or might-have-beens of their life.

Since all states in Australia have passed adoption

information Acts in recent years, it is now possible for adopted children and their birth parents to find out the facts about their past. If you have been adopted or had to give a child up for adoption and you want more information, the first step is to approach the government department in your state responsible for community services. I have listed these individually in Appendix B. They can also put you in touch with a number of other agencies, such as the Post Adoption Resource Centre in Sydney, which gives information as well as offering counselling.

Aboriginal state wards: The taking of Aboriginal children from their families to be made wards of the state caused the traumatic disruption of countless life stories. Many Aborigines find it especially important to write their stories because not only their personal history but also their cultural history has been torn apart.

An agency called Link-Up (NSW) helps Aborigines taken from their families by government departments to reconnect to their past. Link-Up has connections in other states, again listed in Appendix B.

While researching the facts is important, it is only a small part of writing your life story. Life story is not family history, although it will almost certainly include some family history. Neither is it a litany of well-researched facts or a straightforward historical account; it is a personal journey of exploration, exciting and sometimes confronting. Even if you never find out all the facts, the journey itself will be rewarding.

READING

No Place for a Woman

On the tenth day of waiting for the rain to stop at the Number Two Bore, I wrote:

Most of the people around us think we have, er, rooms to let, or that we're elevenpence short of a shilling, leaving in this sort of weather; but we are not alone. A very sad and weary party pulled in here the other day after completing a very boggy and difficult trip from Boroloola. They had an old Dodge truck, and were only bogged twenty-two times!

The driver said to Dad, 'If you take it in this weather, you won't get through; if you do try, you are a plucky lot of fools!'

The next day, after eleven days of waiting, we 'plucky lot of fools' set out once again. It still poured off and on, and we moved when we could and waited it out between storms. We were all getting very tired of the sight of mud, and our rations were low. Some days, we were able to walk faster than the cars could move.

9th March: About every five yards we drop into a gilgai hole. We jack up the wheels—we all have our bit to do—and gather antbeds to be packed under each wheel to give it a firm bottom and grip. All day long we trudge along the track, making very little progress.

A few days later we had the rare sight of another party of travellers:

13th March: We are not the only ones in trouble. We camp on one side of a big blacksoil flat, and on the other side camp another party. One of their tracks is down well and truly. The others gave us some provisions to carry on with, and a small piece of dried corned meat was relished by us all.

The next morning everyone met together to consider how to help each other. By three o'clock that afternoon we eventually got across. Soon after, we reached Daly

Waters Cattle Station and it seemed our struggle with the wet season might be almost over, because the 'knock-'em-down' winds had started—the winds that flatten the grass down, and which are a sign of the approaching dry season.

I reported to my diary on 18th March:

Our rations are even lower. All that the station could oblige us with was a bag of flour. So, to make things last, we made a meal of pigweed (a wild herb grass). It really isn't so bad at all, a bit slimy, that's all.

We only went down two bogs today, and our greatest concern was to know how the eighteen mile plain was. We had been told it was more a sea than a plain, and that our cars would disappear completely out of sight in the mud. Imagine our relief when we reached it and found that the water had practically dried up. Tonight we camped like Robinson Crusoe, on a lonely island. There is water all around us. We are going to camp here for a day.

When we reached Newcastle Waters we were down to a quarter of a bag of flour, one tin of jam, two tins of camp pie, and one of sardines—not much between seven of us. My sandy blight was worse, and very painful. All four children had it now, and poor Mother was having a hard time of it, keeping us all comforted. At least when we started out again we had the relief of knowing we had topped up our food and fuel supplies.

After we left Newcastle Waters Station, we crossed the Blue Bush River and drove on along the track to Powell Creek Station.

We passed a bush grave today, so lonely out here. The stone said: 'Dearly loved and sorely missed.' It had a lovely marble cross on it. It was today twenty-three years ago that the man was buried, 1906. I placed a bunch of wildflowers on it. It said that death had been caused by exposure. What a sad and terrible ending.

This extract is taken from Mayse Young's account of her life in the Northern Territory, *No Place for a Woman,* written with Gabrielle Dalton (Pan Macmillan, 1991). In it she has used entries from a diary she kept during a journey her family made across Australia in 1929 when she was sixteen. She has used the diary indirectly much of the time, drawing on it to refresh her memory, but she has also used direct extracts which bring us right back to a time when travelling in the outback was truly a life and death challenge. She also shares with us the lively awareness of a teenager who treats the hardships as adventure.

The intimacy of a diary involves us in her moods and emotions and helps give us a feel for what the experience was really like. Using the diary gives us the feeling of experiencing her life 'close up'. It is a good way of bringing a particular episode into sharper focus.

WRITING EXERCISES

1 Records

Take an official document of your life. Your birth certificate, adoption papers, a school report, marriage certificate, Social Security card, even a tax notice! Look at it for a while, absorbing its implications, its significance. Think about its associations, the stories connected to it. What has come about because of this document? What went on before it was issued? Who else does it involve? Such innocent-looking items often conceal a world of stories. Write for ten minutes.

2 Mementos

Take a memento of a holiday from any period in your life. A seashell, photograph, postcard. Holidays by their nature involve different places, different people, and are therefore often more memorable than everyday life. Picture yourself on that holiday—the place, the people you met, the clothes you wore, the different feel of holiday living, the sights and smells. I always think of Manly Beach in Sydney and the smell of salty air and coconut oil and fish and chips. Write as much as you can think of about the particular holiday and then about holidays generally.

3 Newspapers

Search in a library for a newspaper account of a public event you remember from childhood. It could be a lost child, the war, a bushfire, the Easter show, a crime or criminal everyone was talking about. Compare your memory of the event with the newspaper account. Write about it, starting with your recollection. This can be used as a way in to writing about the impact of the outside world on your childhood. This is especially important if you want to place your life in the context of a wider world. However private we are, the outside world still affects us and the way we live.

4 Interview

Interview a family member or friend on any topic related to your life. You may learn things you didn't know and the process may also help jog your own memory. Ask them to talk about a particular time that you shared, or a particular person you both knew. Using the results of your interview, write a short piece entitled 'What others have told me'.

LIFE STORY WRITERS

The following piece, by Ann P., was written as a response to the first exercise. It is part of her search for her origins, her desire to look behind the door of her adoption. She has used the adoption papers to help her write about her emotions at various stages of her life. One point that may not be clear: the 'mother' she refers to is her adoptive mother.

Adoption Papers

I remember it as blue, this paper, this clue. Actually, it is a dirty brown colour. It was probably beige back then. Now it has the creases, the yellowing of age. Like me. I smile to myself. Well, it is almost my age. *Order of Adoption in the matter of (strange name, a stranger's name),* followed in brackets by *to be known as Ann. And in the matter of the Child Welfare Act, 1939, Part XIX, blah, blah, blah.*

There follow six columns headed *Particulars of the child proposed to be adopted.* Only one column is filled in. The stranger's name *to be known as Ann, born 19th April, 1951, at Crown Street Women's Hospital, Father's name: Blank, Mother's maiden name: . . . . . . Mother's Christian name: . . . . . .*

There she is!

It is that kind of official paper, with watermarks I can't read. *In the Supreme Court of N.S.W. in Equity No 734* (pencilled in red) *of 1951.*

As I recount this in 1992 I have an abiding image of a lone figure, myself, walking through a cemetery. There are all these gravestones claiming that here, where there is no sign of life, there was life. These stones, however, bear only names, no details. No details of the life, just that it had existed. Yet somehow, it is as though I, the onlooker, am the ghost.

There is so much death in this paper, dealt with quickly, efficiently, by the Machine, administered by strangers.

I remember the day I first held this paper in my hand. I was twelve. I was captivated by my mother's carved wooden box, the mysterious one she kept in the bottom drawer of her dressing table. So, seizing some opportunity afforded by her absence, I invaded. I wish I could say, investigated, but it was pure, unadulterated snooping. I almost said 'invasion of privacy'. How can retrieving information about oneself be an invasion of another's privacy? When you are adopted, any such retrieval is deemed an invasion of privacy. That privacy is guarded zealously by the Law. The fact is that I should never have seen this paper, let alone possessed it. My possession of it I owe to the insight, love and (still) illegal action of my mother. She gave it into my possession when I was in my mid-30s. Then and now I have no legal right to it.

I digress. I was twelve. Deeply religious, deeply distressed, often depressed. The good Catholic girl blossoming into womanhood. Sin lurked everywhere: in our bodies; in our minds; in what we committed and omitted; and, as women, in our very beings. The impure thoughts of men were our doing, their impure actions, our fault. My consolation, my salvation, lay in my absolute devotion, the spiritual nurturance of the Church.

I found the paper. Guilt! I should not see this. I unfold it. I should not do this. My eyes scan to *Mother's maiden name:* . . . . . . *Mother's Christian name:* . . . . . . I drink it in.

My eyes are riveted by the Blank next to *Father's name.* A puzzle of a thousand pieces rushes together in my mind. The princess dies of shame. 'Mortal sin, girls, is the absence of God.' Sister Concepta stared at us, each one of us. Her eyes drilled into me, unleashing the white-hot, searing pain. 'When a person commits a mortal sin, they knowingly banish God from their lives. Girls, don't let yourselves be lured into mortal sin by the promise of mere bodily pleasure . . . blah, blah, blah.' Her voice recedes as the pain forces me out of my body. Somehow, I watch myself from somewhere near the ceiling, the thousand-pieced picture flooding my mind with the answers to a thousand questions. I am not supposed to be here! God did not plan me! I was conceived in God's absence. There is no plan for me. In a microsecond, my dis-ease, my loneliness, my aloneness were explained.

The second piece was written after a number of interviews led Gloria R. to her father, whom she had not seen for 30 years. She uses dialogue to dramatically convey the emotion of the events that followed.

A Unique Experience

I had telephoned in trepidation, not knowing the response I would get from the other end. When I asked to speak to R.K., the young female voice yelled: 'Dad! It's for you.'

'Who is it?'

'A Gloria Rogers.' My heart was thundering. I felt weak as I heard footsteps and the sound of whispering in the background.

'Hello, Dad, this is Gloria, your eldest daughter. If you don't want to speak to me it's OK.'

'No, no, *marginj* (daughter), it's all right. Speak to me.' More whispering in the background, female and male voices this time.

My father and I talked for almost two hours that first time (what a phone bill next time), both of us wanting to know and absorb every piece of information, trying to fill a void of 30 years' absence. He had remarried back into the Aboriginal community, and lost his second wife some years ago.

I spoke to the brothers and sisters that I had not known existed. Two brothers, two sisters, voices shy and hesitant and just a little bewildered. Later, feeling exhilarated, I sat down to write my father a letter. Where to start? I wanted to tell him everything—about his grandchildren and the good man I married, all about my life—but I also wanted to ask him so many questions. It was a letter full of questions. That was three months ago. Recently my husband and I finalised plans to visit him for the first time when we both would have holidays. So why am I constantly thinking of him, day and night? And why is that damn willy wagtail hanging around my back door calling out and getting agitated every time I go outside? Three days it's been there now, wagging its tail this way and that. Every morning there he is again.

'What's wrong with you *gitra gitra* (wagtail)? Shoo, shoo, go away, you are starting to spook me. SHOOO!'

'Mum! Aunty Iris is on the phone, she sounds upset,' said my teenage daughter.

'Hello Aunty?'

'Hello, Glory. I have some very bad news for you, I'm afraid.' My heart was pounding, and the phone suddenly felt heavy as I tried to concentrate. 'I'm sorry dear, I had a phone call just a while ago. Your Dad died . . . Glory, Glory, are you still there? Are you all right?'

'Yes, Aunty, I'm OK. What happened? He seemed fine when I spoke to him a couple of days ago. He was telling me how much he was looking forward to our visit.'

'I don't know, love, he had a hard life after the divorce. Maybe he was just worn out by time. I knew something bad was to happen to a family member anyway, because your grandmother's picture fell off the wall yesterday, and the willy wagtails have been bothering me for days.'

I didn't know what Aunty meant, although I always knew she was superstitious. It was only after my father's funeral that an Aboriginal elder told me that willy wagtails are regarded as news bringers (good or bad).

[Note: I used my father's initials, R.K., as there is an Aboriginal belief which forbids the use of the name of a deceased person.]

Turn to the next workshop for a discussion of memory and how to retrieve those elusive moments of your life.

6
Workshop III: Memory

An unused memory gets lost, ceases to exist, dissolves into nothing—an alarming thought. Consequently, the faculty to preserve, to remember, must be developed.

Christa Wolf

WHEN I WAS a child I had four maiden great-aunts. Of the six daughters in their family, one died at the age of eleven, one, my grandmother, married and had children, and the other four remained single and childless. They lived together in a dark Victorian house in which each bedroom still had a pitcher and basin for bathing. My mother said the aunts used to empty their hot-water bottles into the basins in the morning. It was just the right temperature to wash their faces before they stepped out into the harsh morning light of their country town.

The aunts had no children to tell their lives to; they did not keep journals and did not take part in public life.

There is no record anywhere of the thoughts, feelings, personal achievements of all their long lives in that shadowy house on the western plains. When the last person who remembers them dies, it will be as if they had never lived. In fact, my mother remarked that one of the aunts, Allie, said those exact words to her: 'When I die, it will be as if I had never lived.'

Their lives will have dissolved into nothing . . . Like Christa Wolf, I am alarmed by that thought. To have been through the pain and joy of life, to have seen the sun rise when no-one else was awake, to have smelled lilacs in the evening; then for it all to vanish like water poured into sand.

We have the wonderful capacity of memory to ensure that things don't just happen and then disappear without trace. In Greek mythology, Memory, known as Mnemosyne, is the mother of the Muses, the creative spirits of humankind. In other words, memory is the mother of creativity. Lives are important and memories are the vital echoes of our lives. If we lost our memories we would not know ourselves. It is up to us to use our memories. With a few easy techniques they can be more and more easily recalled and written down.

How does memory work? The *Macquarie Dictionary* says memory is 'the mental faculty of retaining and retrieving impressions'. So there are two essential functions, storage and retrieval. If memories were merely stored and could not be retrieved, they would be of no use.

In fact, many people feel that they do have memories stored somewhere—if only they could release them. The written responses to memory exercises I have given in workshops have convinced me that you can recall memories you believe are lost. Even people who are sure they have no recollection of a particular period or person are astonished and delighted to find memories flooding back.

This observation is backed up by what little scientific knowledge we have about the workings of memory. The basic operations of memory are the gathering, storing and recalling of impressions of events, people and sensations. The first, easily lost imprint of memory is recorded by the cells' bioelectrical action. Storing, the changeover to long-term memory, is probably a chemical operation. Our memories thus become part of our biological make-up. We are, literally, made of our memories.

For all that, our memories are notoriously unreliable. We are sometimes sure we remember events that can be proved not to have happened. The American writer Mary McCarthy told of how for years one of her children believed Mussolini had been thrown off a bus in Connecticut! When she was older and realised it couldn't have happened she questioned her mother about the incident. It turned out that she had been waiting at a bus stop with her mother when a bus pulled up and a man got out. At the same time, the bus driver leaned over and called out, 'Mussolini has been thrown out.'

I suspect that in your own family there are contradictory versions of the same event, and everyone is sure their version is the correct one. 'I can see it now,' the person exclaims, and becomes irritated when the picture in their mind is questioned or denied. Unlike Mary McCarthy's story, few family memories can be verified. You can argue for hours but you will not persuade someone to change what they 'remember'. I once heard a story from a younger sister; even when her older sister triumphantly said, 'But you can't have been there, you weren't even born then,' she still insisted her account was correct.

If you have a memory which is plain as day to you and contradicted by others, check your facts as much as you are able. Talk to others who may have been there at the time. Try to line the memory up with a public event of the time to check the date. Even play music from the time and try to picture the surroundings of the memory. If everything fails and you are still sure of a memory that no-one else agrees with, hold onto it. It is your memory, it is the way you experienced the event, and so it is your truth. Write it down. If you are concerned that others may be hurt, add a rider to the effect that others may query this version if they wish, but this is the way you remember things.

The most intriguing aspect of memory is that it is selective. In fact, the unreliable and contradictory nature of memory is largely due to this mysterious selection process. We remember some things and we appear to forget others. It seems there are some events, people, sensations, that our memories select for storage and easy recall, and others that are apparently discarded.

I remember one morning in primary school when my teacher stood over me. I can hear the disdain in his voice but I cannot see his features except for his receding gingery hair. He is wearing brown clothes—I still dislike brown clothes on gingery men. He has dry, chalky fingers as he holds mine and cleans my fingernails in front of the whole school, saying, 'Take your dirt back to your farm.' The scissors scrape under my nails and my face burns red. 'Ugghh,' says the teacher. He shakes his shiny clean shoe, pretending that the dirt from my nails has fallen on it. Even then I knew it hadn't really, but his gesture still had the desired effect of increasing my humiliation.

It's easy to see why this apparently minor incident was remembered, even after many years. The teacher almost certainly would not recall the incident, but the humiliated child does. It isn't always so obvious why we remember some things and not others, but I have found that if we have a strong memory of a particular thing, it is very likely that it has some deeper significance for us. Often the memory may seem random, inconsequential, but when you look at it more closely you will discover that it relates to or illuminates another aspect of your life.

A workshop student wrote of an incident from her early childhood, when her family lived in a flat on a dim laneway lined with garbage bins in Sydney's Kings Cross. She was in her mother's arms as she answered the door. There was a woman standing there in a shaft of light. She does not remember what the woman looked like or what she wanted, but she does remember how beautiful the shaft of light in the shadowy alley was. She would have been less than two years old when she experienced this delight in beauty.

She thought the memory was inconsequential, but as we talked about it, she realised that she had always responded to natural phenomena, beauty and light, more than she did to people. For 60 years she had retained from babyhood a memory of seemingly no importance which was, in fact, a symbol of the way she'd lived her whole life.

I do not suggest that all your memories have a deep or symbolic significance, but consider them carefully, especially the ones that prompt you to exclaim, 'Now, why do I remember that?' You may find that you do so for a good reason.

Memory, like the unconscious, often works through symbols that operate through imaginative association rather than logic. This can make the significance of some memories difficult to unravel. Your memory is a poet; it enjoys symbols. Write down what your memory has kept for you. Its meanings will emerge as you continue with your life story.

You may have noticed that I said 'appear to forget' and 'apparently discarded [from memory]'. I am not sure that any experience is forgotten altogether. Many workshop students have claimed to have no memories of certain periods in their life only to find a flood of memories once they open a tiny 'gate' in their minds. Because of this, I am inclined to believe that everything that happens to us is stored in memory and that it is only our selective retrieval system that prevents us from having access to it.

How to remember

So how do you open this 'gate' in the mind? The answer lies in the way in which memories are stored. We all know that certain sensations, especially smells, will bring back events as if we were there. This means that sensory experience is stored 'alongside' our impressions of events—the two are associated. All memories, in fact, are stored in association with other memories. So it is that one memory can trigger another—especially, I have found, if you write it down. The very act of writing seems to unsettle the apparently silent spaces around the memory and nudge other memories out into the light. Some suggestions for retrieving memories are:

- Listen to the music of the era you want to recall and let it 'take you away'.
- Gaze intently at photographs taking in all the details; try photographs of places as well as people from your past.
- Take a trip back to where you used to live; if you are lucky you may even be able to go inside.
- Take a trip to your old school or workplace; look at the physical details with care because they will jog memories of how you felt and what you thought.
- Re-read books you read in the past; books from childhood are especially powerful in their associations.
- Go to the library and read old newspapers; select both local and national papers and remember to look at the advertisements as well.
- Talk with family members and old friends; they can often remember fragments that will jog your memory.
- Touch old dresses or favourite ornaments—it's amazing what our finger-tips, indeed, all our senses can remember.
- Smell fragrances, perfumes, flowers; any smells which you associate with particular times in your life.

There are some memories that we would rather not retrieve. They may be too painful or too hurtful to others or simply too embarrassing to recall. You may decide you do not want to write about them. This is always your decision. If you want to let memories lie undisturbed, you are free to do so. Still, it is true that facing memories again can lessen their power to disturb.

A number of workshop students have written about distressing memories—of childhood abuse, adoption, the death of a parent, parental divorce—which they had previously left unexamined. All but one have said that writing down those memories gave them a sense of release. The one who didn't said the memories of violence against her mother were still too disturbing and she decided not to continue her writing. (She did, however, keep coming to class.) It was her decision and it is certainly yours if you wish to let some memories lie. You alone will know if you are ready to face the emotions they may stir up.

Memories can be emotional. They can also be sensual or symbolic. Sometimes it is the feeling of joy or fear we remember, sometimes the smell or sound, sometimes a clear image. We may remember a whole sequence of events, or just a tantalising fragment. Exploring and writing down your memories can be one of the most exciting journeys of your life.

READING

The Road from Coorain

My first steps were taken in a household in which the hard domestic chores were performed by men under my mother's eagle-eyed supervision. Because of my mother's orderliness, the household had an unbreakable routine so that I can tell from this early memory what day of the week it was. On Monday the laundry was done. White things were boiled in the copper and starched. Colored things were scrubbed by hand and rinsed in blue. Care was taken in hanging them out to dry lest the sun bleach the colored fabrics white. On Tuesdays the ironing was done with flatirons heated on top of the kitchen stove. As the household grew, the whole of Wednesday was needed for sewing and mending. Thursday was for baking. Scones, cupcakes, sponge and pound cakes for tea, tarts and flans for desserts, meat pies to use up leftovers. All were baked in the oven of the wood stove, with a quick test of the hand to determine whether the oven was 'just right' to brown pastry or make a sponge cake rise. Friday was for cleaning house. Every room was swept and dusted thoroughly, every floor was washed, wax polish was applied to the linoleum floors, and then they were shone by hand. On the Friday of my first steps, this task was being done by Jimmie Walker, a cheerful and willing Irish lad in his late teens. Jimmie had been sent out by an emigrants' welfare organisation to find his fortune in Australia. He was desperately homesick when he came to Coorain, and loved to play with us children because we reminded him of his brothers and sisters back home. We were entranced with a new playmate and were always by his side as he worked. His metabolism was attuned to gentler climates and we children were astonished and fascinated by the extent of his perspiration compared with that of the hard-bitten Australians we knew. On this Friday I was assisting the floor polishing by crawling backwards in front of him, ever alert to the point when a river of perspiration would drop from his forehead and nose and smear the beauty of the floor he was polishing. While we were thus engaged, he on hands and knees, and I crawling backwards intently observing his forehead, I suddenly stood erect and went to fetch a fresh towel for dealing with the flood. I don't recall the steps, but I have a clear picture of the excited faces of my mother and brothers summoned by Jimmie's shout.

Another of my earliest memories is of my mother singing me to sleep seated on a cane chair on the front verandah of the house. She and I, and the governess instructing my brothers in a nearby room, were a tiny island of women in a world that revolved around male activities. Her voice was cheerful, positive and relaxed as she hugged me warmly. I recall the comfort and security of being sung to sleep and also some tentative efforts to struggle out of the warm embrace. I was born with a different type of skin and hair from the rest of the family. Their hair grew luxuriantly and curled. Mine was fine and limply straight. They tanned in the sun. I freckled and grew scarlet. The tweed coat my mother was wearing as she cradled me scratched and prickled so that mixed in with the security was a sense of being ill at ease. The memory is symbolic of the way our relationship was to unfold.

This extract is from the second chapter of *The Road from Coorain*, by Jill Ker Conway (Alfred A. Knopf, Inc., 1989), which tells of her journey from an outback sheep station in western New South Wales to academic life in the United States. This piece shows how a small fragment of memory can be used to explore a much wider area. From the author's memory of her first steps we learn much about daily life in the homestead, about the social conditions of the time and about the character of her mother. Let your first memory flow into other areas in this way. This autobiography is also well worth reading for its wonderful descriptions, for its insights into a mother–daughter relationship, and for its discussions of the England–Australia connection.

WRITING EXERCISES

1 First memory

Consider your very first memory. Go as far back as you can. Write down everything you remember, what you can see, feel, smell, hear. Let this memory flow on to other events it reminds you of, other people who may have been there, the surroundings as you now know they were. Remember, your memory is a poet, let it have its say. Write for ten minutes.

2 House plan

Take a pencil or crayon and draw a map of the house you lived in around the age of seven. Spend about five minutes drawing it as accurately as you can. Then take a few minutes to mentally wander through the house you have drawn. Go in through the door and have a look around. Go from room to room. As soon as you see something that catches your interest for any reason, stop. And start writing. Write about what you see, or what happened there, or who you've bumped into. Write for ten minutes from the time something catches your attention.

This is a fascinating exercise because you will most probably find that the memory you have accessed dates from when you were seven to ten years old. This is the age when you start drawing maps of your house or your room or your district, the age when you start thinking

71

conceptually about your place in the world. You can do this exercise dozens of times, going into a different room each time. Vary it by drawing a map of your bedroom. Or a map of your schoolyard or backyard. You will probably find you know the backyard of the house where you lived when you were seven better than you know your own backyard now.

3 Take an object

Take an object that comes from the time in your life you want to write about. A childhood toy, a schoolbook, an ornament, a kitchen table. Look at it carefully, touch it, let your mind wander over the associations this object has for you. If nothing comes freely to mind, start by describing its physical appearance, when you first acquired it or its history. Soon you will find that other things are jostling to be written. Ten minutes.

4 Music

Select some music that is characteristic of a particular period of your life. Perhaps it was played on the wireless, or came from a film or a record you played frequently. Listen to the music and let the faces and feelings of the time come back. Have a notebook handy and jot down whatever comes up. Take one of the people or events you have made a note of and write about them. You can also use music in association with most of the other exercises. Music is a great gatherer of memories.

LIFE STORY WRITERS

The following piece, by Bob P., is an extract from a chapter of his life story. It developed from his writing about his first memory. He has built on the memory to create a moving story of early childhood.

Entry and Exit

Our two small heads looked up into the inky blackness. The darkness was broken by the light streaming from the door of the room as Dad's head appeared.

'Don't make any more noise—shh—you've got a baby brother!' The head disappeared then quickly reappeared. 'He's called Harold,' he said in a loud whisper, then it was dark again.

The next few days were spent in a whirl of people and events. I still had not been able to see Harold or Mother. Even though I asked so many questions, there never seemed to be any satisfying answers. Now that I had a baby brother, I was happy, but Mary, my sister, did not seemed to be pleased at all. Twice I caught her crying. She had been sent around to Auntie Mary's to stay. Relatives came and went and most of them were in tears too. I asked about Harold, as I had not heard him crying, only to be told that he also had gone to Auntie Mary's, just for the time being.

The following day I came into the house to find Dad leaning with his head on the mantelpiece with his head on his arms. 'I wish I was dead. I wish I was dead,' he kept saying. He must have realised suddenly that I was there and turned around to face me. I noticed that his eyes were red. I asked if I could see Mother, but he just mumbled something and quickly left the room.

It was all rather confusing and there had been other strange things happening of late. For one thing, I had come in from play to find some men taking something up the stairs; I was not sure what it was as it was covered by a sheet, but it looked awfully like a box.

When I asked them about it I was ushered out to play. What I did notice was that the door of Mother's bedroom had been sealed all around with white paper. Why did all those people keep looking at me and mumbling, particularly Mrs Francis from across the road; she had given me a penny for no apparent reason, and I thought she was still cross with me since I had broken her window with a ball a few days ago.

One morning I was taken to stay with Auntie Hannah, a few doors away. I was given some sweets and a comic and told to stay indoors. It was so bewildering. On a nice day like this they usually told me to go outside and play in no uncertain terms, especially when Mother wanted to get on with her work. Also, why were Auntie Hannah's front blinds drawn? Come to think of it, so were the blinds of some of the other houses in the street.

After lunch, Dad called for me and took me home. We entered the front door to find quite a number of people inside the front room, mostly neighbours, but one or two strangers were there. Some of the ladies had handkerchiefs to their faces and did not look very happy. I ran over to Dad and stood by his side. It was then I saw the long yellow box on a stand over by the fireplace. One of those horrible coffins I used to go with Mother to see. In front were bunches of flowers, very pretty, but I hated them because they smelled sort of sickly. People began to walk by the box and as they passed Dad they shook his hand and muttered something. Quite a few neighbours mumbled some words to me but I couldn't understand what they said, whilst one or two pressed coins into my hand. This was great, I thought, as I looked down at the coins. There was even a small silver one, too. I was not taking too much notice of the proceedings as I was more concerned about what I could buy. Sweets, chocolates—oh yes, a 'Lucky Bag' for Mary, there were all sorts in those. Dad liked 'England's Own', the chocolate caramels. What about Harold? Well, maybe a lollypop for him to lick would do. Yes, and Mother, what about her? I looked up at Dad and said, 'Where's Mother?'

There was a hush as all the mumbling stopped and everyone looked at me, then turned their gaze to Dad. There was a few seconds' silence, and then Dad picked me up and walked over to the fireplace where the box was.

I looked down and there was Mother in a white dress, looking very pale. I leaned towards her and said, 'Mother—what—' Dad cut me short.

'Shh—Bobby—Mother's dead. She's gone to heaven.'

Dad put me down. There was a silence. Dead? I felt like I wanted to cry but didn't. Mother had told me about those people in coffins. They were only shells and the real people had gone to heaven and were happy. I remembered that boy on Whalley Road who had gone to heaven. He was in one of those boxes and he had a sore on his lip.

'When will she come back from heaven, Dad?'

Dad looked at me and said, 'In a while. Now why don't you go out and play.' Outside in the sunlight I thought about Mother being in heaven and wondered when I would see her again. I didn't feel too sad as my mind was really on the sweets. My problem was deciding what to buy from the corner shop; Mrs Hickson had such a good selection—toffee potatoes and peas, liquorice allsorts, Pomfret Cakes, Fry's chocolate bars, sugared almonds, dolly mixtures, liquorice pipes, tiger nuts . . . so many things to choose from.

In bed that night I thought again about Mother. I knew I would see her again, but it was hard to decide how long it might be. One week, two weeks, or would it be before Christmas, because that was such a long way off. Then I remembered something else.

'Dad! Dad!' I called downstairs.

Dad came running up the stairs. 'What is it, son?'

I reached down for my trousers at the foot of the bed and dug into one of the pockets. I brought out what was now a tangle of sticky sweets.

'Here's Mother's sweets, I forgot.'

Turn to the next workshop, on structure, for ideas on how to start joining together all the different pieces of your life story.

7
Workshop IV: Structure

It will all come together, I am sure, like the pieces
of a mosaic or the scattered chips in a kaleidoscope.

George Johnston

LIKE A MOSAIC artist, or a bowerbird with
his kingfisher feathers and bits of willow-ware plate and
cicada shells, you have gathered your memories together.
They lie tumbled in a heap, a treasure-house of your life
with a light now shining on it, catching some memories
and making them glow. Some you have written down
and some are still waiting to be written. You are probably
starting to wonder, how can I arrange all this? How can
I organise it?

You could just leave it as a random collection of
memories, a pile of bits and pieces. But it seems there
is an impulse in humans, as well as in bowerbirds, that
makes us want to order our experience according to some
kind of underlying principle.

Alexander Pope, the eighteenth-century poet, said, 'Order is Heav'n's first law'. Well, yes, but the eighteenth century had a passion for order, with no idea that chaos also has its patterns. Order does not have to be rigid, though even a kaleidoscope does not form its shapes at random. There is a geometry behind the way the brightly coloured pieces fall and arrange themselves, a structure that orders the pieces.

WHY STRUCTURE?

Organising your material, or structuring it, makes it easier to manage. Scientists, for example, structure vast amounts of information into categories to make it easier to remember and analyse. In writing, too much random information is difficult to read with sustained interest.

Finding or giving structure is a way of creating meaning. Some argue that structure is created so that meaning may be created; others believe that structure and meaning are inherent in life. Either way, we depend on structure to make sense of our lives.

Structure, as the word suggests, is also what makes your writing 'hang together'. If you take out a structural wall in a building, there is a good chance the building will fall down. Without some kind of structure holding it together, your writing may become fragmented and give the impression that it is falling apart.

Finally, structure is inherently pleasing. We find a curious delight in order and rhythmic recurrence.

HOW TO STRUCTURE

The bowerbird instinctively structures his material

according to the theme of the colour blue. It is not quite so easy for us; we can choose from a variety of structures, or organising principles.

Chronology

This is the most usual way of structuring a life story. It simply means arranging your material in a chronological sequence, that is, starting at your birth and continuing year by year until the present. Most people don't remember their life year by year, so they opt for periods.

A simple division of life into periods is: birth and early childhood (up to 5 years old); middle childhood (6–13); teenage years (14–20); Early adulthood (20–30); middle years (30–60); later years (60 onwards).

A similar division, still chronological, is according to major life events such as: marriage of parents; birth; arrival of brothers and sisters; starting school; making friends; moving house; starting high school; first job; marriage; children; professional life. This is a hypothetical life—your life may not fit this pattern at all. Work out a chronology of major life events that suits you.

There are other chronological divisions you can use. If, for example, you have moved house often, you could use your stays in each house as the divisions. Instead of middle childhood as a section you might have Ipswich house 1941–45; Pepper St, Brisbane 1946–47; George St, Brisbane 1947–50. This may be a more natural way for you to organise your material, as it parallels the way you have stored it in your memory.

If you are treating your life story as a social history, as 'sociography rather than autobiography' as Donald Horne put it, you may want to use historical periods as your chronological divisions. You could use divisions such as the Depression; the Second World War; the postwar years; the 60s boom, and so on. In this way you will be able to emphasise the events of your life as influenced by, and in the context of, a wider history.

The chronological divisions you use will depend on your own life. Your memory has probably already developed its own divisions as it has silently gone about its business of storing information. Try to discern its chronological divisions and use them in your writing.

In life, events rarely happen one after the other. Many things happen at once and it is often difficult to tell when events begin and end. A strict chronology just doesn't apply, but chronology needn't be a stiff, artificial order. It can be made to ebb and flow, to race forward to the end of an episode and then back to the start of an event running parallel to it. It can be flexible as well as straightforward and easy to use.

Topics

You may not want to write your life chronologically, but as a series of selected events that are particularly interesting. In that case, arranging your material by topic would be more useful. With this kind of structure you write only about the particular aspects of your life that come under the topic headings. You are not concerned with chronological order, you just want to cover important aspects of your life as you have experienced them. The topics you choose depend completely on what you discern as important in your life. They may be based on an aspect of your inner life, such as a delight in nature; particular people, such as a beloved grandparent; interesting individuals you have met; or exciting events you have been involved in.

You can combine a few large topic areas with lots of smaller topics. Look at *Out of Africa,* by Karen Blixen (Century, 1985), to see how she uses the overall subject of her years in Africa to provide the basic structure and then divides it into five large topic areas. These are further divided into a patchwork of sub-topics discussed at varying lengths, some for only a paragraph, some for several pages. In this way Blixen places a wide variety of people into a framework to create an intricate picture of her experiences in Africa. She does not impose chronology or plot, but makes a collage.

Themes

Themes are the underlying issues or ideas in writing. In a life story, as in fiction, they are revealed in patterns of action and in images. Remember at school when you were studying Shakespeare and explored the theme of *Macbeth*, for example, by looking for examples of his 'ambition' in the drama? You follow a similar process here, except that the drama is your own life, which may not be as violent as Macbeth's but is probably just as complex.

When you look at your life you may notice that a particular experience keeps recurring. Perhaps you have had to start again a number of times in your life. You could say that 'new beginnings' seems to be a theme of your life. Or if you keep falling in love with the 'wrong' person, you may see that as the theme of your life. Maybe 'reaching for the stars' is your theme, or 'never giving up'.

81

You can use your theme, or themes, to decide what to put in and what to leave out. Instead of including everything you can think of, include only those experiences that relate to the themes.

There are a number of themes common to many lives—friendship, love, renewal, the search for self-knowledge, appreciation of beauty, being an outsider, overcoming obstacles. Use whichever themes apply to your life to help you shape your material.

Remember, themes do not exist of themselves. They are abstract ideas and are manifested through events, people or images. You will convey your themes in the stories that you choose to write. If you write about these themes directly, try to avoid being either too vague or too preachy.

Themes and chronology can be combined. These structures do not have to be mutually exclusive. Most writers use a number of different structures.

A particular period

You may decide that you want to write about just one episode in your life in great detail. This is often the choice when you have experienced life-changing events such as a divorce, or the birth of a child, or a severe illness, or a 'road to Damascus' illumination. Nothing happens in a vacuum, but the lead-up to the episode, the experience itself and its repercussions set natural limits, which at least give you the basic shape of your story.

You may choose to write only about your childhood, or about a period spent in a foreign country, or any other specific period. This makes it easier to know what to include, but within any given period you still need to organise your material. In Workshop V I suggest some plot structures that may be of use if you are writing about a particular period.

As I noted in Workshop II, it can be most interesting to keep a journal while you are writing your life story. In it you can record your difficulties, the discovery process, your changing feelings as you write about your life. This journal can be more than interesting: it can also help you structure your life story. You can use extracts from your journal to connect the various pieces of your life story together. Your life story then becomes a combination of the past and the present. The past is stitched together using the journal of the present.

For example, you may have found some old letters that you would like to use in your life story. In your journal you write about how you felt looking at these letters again and how uncertain you are about using them. Put that discussion from your journal into your life story to create a 'frame' for the letters. In this way, the journal of the present creates a continuity, joining the pieces of your past together.

READING

Poppy

Poppy had a habit, which Richard teased, and China criticised, of plaiting scraps of wool, cotton, thin strips of material, hair ribbon, crepe paper and anything else at hand, into a thick multi-coloured twine. This she rolled into balls which she stored in the bottom drawer of the Welsh dresser China had given her and Richard for their wedding. She used the threads to tie papers, letters and old school reports into manageable bundles, or to wrap presents, or to hook a doorknob to a peg in the wall to stop it banging in the wind. It was a habit she developed as a child during the Depression, or soon after, though it was generated less by economic than inner needs, the anxieties and insecurities of a child growing up in a rich, godless home.

When she died, there was a ball of this twine in the drawer beside her bed. There was also a small enamel-lidded box of scraps that were still to be plaited. And although it was a habit which had irritated May, Phoebe and me for years, we couldn't bring ourselves to throw any of it out. We each took some, picking through it carefully to make our choice. The rest we packed into boxes and gave to the Day Centre for young offenders which Poppy had started when she finished her training and moved to town, a working woman, no longer married. I've no idea what they did with it. Not having the memories which hampered us, they probably threw it out.

I don't regret the balls of braid which I lugged up to London and then across the world with the rest of my share of the things we cleared from her house. I used it to tie the diaries and letters into bundles to stop them overflowing, off my desk and through the door into the rest of the house, taking over the life I have here, away from her, the family and the history that I'm cautiously unravelling. And though it's faded now, and frayed in parts, for May, Phoebe and me this twine has become a kind of joke, a metaphor Poppy made for her own life: Ariadne's thread. When she heard the story of Ariadne and her labyrinth, she was in Crete where she'd been sent on a holiday paid for by Richard who stayed behind to work, in the hope that she'd recover from her breakdown and the blank years in hospital. It was 1961, and she said it was exactly how she felt she'd lived her life, with a ball of twine in her hands so that other people could find their way.

Is that the feminine condition, always a life-line to other people's lives and therefore split from our own? Who holds the thread for us? Who held it for her? Does this explain the dreams women have: the perfect husband, the perfect lover: priest, guardian, father. Failing that, or perhaps most of all: the perfect mother.

When I look closely at Poppy's braided twine, I fancy I can recognise scraps from dresses I wore more than thirty years ago, hair ribbons given to Phoebe or May, the trim of a blue organdie night-dress, wool from Richard's gardening cardigan. There are other balls of twine made entirely of colours and fabrics I don't recognise, made from the life she lived away from me, clues to memories I can't have. Sometimes I think I should have kept every ball of it, and then all I'd have to do would be to trace the twine back, thread by thread, back to the first knot. Maybe if I knew why the child Poppy made that knot I'd understand all that was necessary for the biography of my mother.

Drusilla Modjeska's book *Poppy* (McPhee Gribble, 1990) is not, strictly speaking, her own life story, but in writing her mother's life she has necessarily written a great deal about her own. Her voice in the present weaves or plaits together all the pieces from her mother's past. In this extract she gives the symbolic plot structure of the book: the plait or braid. This is only one of the patterns of this multi-structured book; it is also structured around a number of themes such as Work, Love and Faith, as well as being very broadly chronological with many leaps back and forward in time and place. The braided plot structure suits the story of Poppy, and the stories of many women's lives, which do not follow one path single-mindedly but must weave in and out of other people's lives. If you are interested in trying out different kinds of structures in your life story, have a look at this book.

WRITING EXERCISES

1 Getting organised

Think carefully about the various structures I have suggested in this workshop: chronological divisions; topics; themes; the journal. Decide which one suits you best and start arranging your pieces. If you have already written a number of pieces in earlier exercises, or even if you only have headings, put them in order according to the structure you have chosen. For example, if you have chosen chronological divisions according to periods of life, put all your childhood pieces together, all your schooldays pieces together, and so on.

Now write a page explaining how you want to organise your material and why, choosing one or more of the structures I have suggested. Write it as a letter to yourself. This is a very good way of thinking through the structure of your life story. It will probably be difficult, because it forces you to take an overview, but once you have done it, you will have a clearer sense of direction in your writing.

2 Time line

Give yourself only ten minutes to write a strict chronology of your life. Start with whatever you think of first and continue with whatever you think of next. The only rule is that it should all be in chronological order. Look at what you have included. If you are lucky you will have drawn up the outline of your life story structure with a minimum of fuss. On the other hand, you may have written only about the public events of your life, and not what was really important to you. If so, try the fourth exercise.

3 Turning points

Write a list of what seem to you to be turning points in your life. Select one of them and write about it for half an hour. You can keep doing this exercise until you have written about all the turning points. In fact, you could organise your whole life story around turning points.

4 I have/have not

This is one of my favourite exercises and it is based on a discussion in which the English poet Robert Graves catalogues what he has and has not done. He lists an odd assortment of activities and facts and achievements and failures, from having walked near Mt Etna when it was erupting to having been questioned for a murder he did not commit. The exercise is to write continuously, for ten minutes, a catalogue of what you have and have not done in your life. Write everything you think of and don't cross anything out. Don't worry if something like 'I have never sung at Covent Garden' comes out. The odd things that come into your head when you haven't got time to prepare can be real indicators of the underlying concerns of your life. They can point the way to the most important stories. When you look at your list you may see a recurring pattern, which is the central story.

An extension of this exercise is to take one item from your list and expand on it.

LIFE STORY WRITERS

In response to the fourth exercise, Petra C. wrote the following list and then expanded on one item. She has written her whole journey to Australia around the idea of tasting her first pineapple. Taking a different approach like this can make your writing fresh and original.

A Catalogue

I have been around the world on a ship and by plane, but I have not yet flown in a glider or a helicopter.
I have learned to dance but failed to grasp Physical Culture.
I have gone to school on a bike in a snowstorm and have come home in a car in a heatwave.
I ate my very first fresh pineapple in Tahiti and loved it and an oyster at the Barrier Reef and hated it.
I have been on a swing that went right over.
I have followed soccer and the Tour de France but never Rugby League.
I learned to drive at 29.
I lived on a bike for 24 years before that.
I analysed Vegemite for Kraft and never could stand it.

I Ate my First Fresh Pineapple in Tahiti

I ate my first fresh pineapple in Tahiti. Doesn't that seem something really simple! Never judge an apple by its skin. Eating pineapple may be simple enough, preparing for it is far from simple, as anybody who has ever fought a pineapple with a knife would know only too well.

This time was no different. Preparations began in May 1964, and the eating occurred on 9 March 1965.

It started with an advertisement in the local Leiden paper, announcing that the Australian government wished to offer a cheap working holiday in Australia to some 200 young Dutch that year. At the same time, Aunt Antoinette, who had provided me in my teens with an, at times, much needed home away from home, arrived for a visit from Australia after migrating there ten years before with her husband and eleven of my cousins.

With that, and a private interview with an immigration officer because of a mistake in the advertisement, the scene was set for the good ship *Flavia* to set out for Australia on a cold, bleak winter's day, with Petronella Johanna Maria van Schijindel and some 1300 others on board.

Rotterdam, Bremerhaven, Tilbury, and hurry, hurry, into the Atlantic to outpace a violent late winter storm. Anyone prone to seasickness stayed in bed, but a small group of the Youthprogramme had a ball. We had a top time on the empty topdeck, while the *Flavia* dipping better than any Big Dipper for at least a week. Clouds and spray were flying, and using unbuttoned jackets for sails, we flew too on the tilting deck.

At last the storm abated and we sailed into calmer waters. And out came the sun and the other passengers. I misjudged the strength of the sun in the cooling breeze and landed in bed with sunstroke, which is not to be preferred over seasickness.

Eleven days of wind and water and we heard the cry, 'Land in sight!' Central America appeared as a haze on the far horizon.

Curacao, and we glided through town. It was

delightful, an old Dutch town dressed up for the hot summer in white and pastels. The sun glared off the friendly Dutch gables. A hot walk from the port, some wide-eyed sightseeing, and a ride in a huge American car with a black driver, and on we sailed.

Through the Panama Canal with its leafy green walls on either side, to Bilbao. It was the weekend before Lent and the time for a farewell to meat, i.e. Carnival. Heeding the advice over the ship's loudspeaker not to carry any valuables, very little money and to move in groups, some of us crammed into another large American car and took off for an amazing tour of the town. None of us was interested in the nightclub, but when we spotted some people dancing in a square, we insisted on stopping there and then.

I have often wondered why the cabbie protested so vigorously. Was he concerned about our safety or his own pocket? Fact is that we did not come to any harm. Instead, we took part in the good-humoured neighbourly folk dancing. A small band played some interesting flutes and drums, augmented by a lot of hand-clapping and vocal encouragement for musicians and dancers alike.

Back on board, the next excitement was breakfast on the Pacific Ocean. For thirteen days we steadily proceeded on this great sea, with nothing to look at but the wake of the ship, the wonderful swell of the long waves, schools of newly polished small silver flying fish, splendid sunsets and sunrises, and in between them, the nights with an ever-changing moon riding the dark sky and throwing sparkles on the dark moving waves. A year later I was reminded of that moonlit darkness when travelling in a coach across the dark-soil plains of Australia's north.

Two days after King Neptune's chaotic messy visit

from his palace at the bottom of the Equator, brought our next encounter with land. The famous Tahiti, the beautiful, would experience our arrival. And what an arrival it was for this group of northern Europeans! Coming from lands where nature hibernates for some five months of the year, and where the sun shines shyly through a moist veil, they stepped onto an island of warm sunshine and never-stopping growth. The narrow dirt streets were overgrown with tree-sized potplants. Little traffic and sunshine and smiles appeared the everyday conditions of life.

Wandering around, we came to a shady airy building which turned out to be the markets. It was full of people and produce and too overwhelming to remember in detail.

But then . . . LOOK! REAL PINEAPPLES! How we all wanted to experience the taste of fresh pineapple. I had only ever had it from a tin at Christmas in a Bavarois. But none of us had any idea how to prepare it. Desire made us pluck up our courage, and using our best French, we asked the young woman if she would prepare it for us. I still remember both the big smile and the large knife.

Fresh pineapple, prepared by a smiling Tahitian, is heavenly!

This piece, by Bettine S., is about a turning point in her life in the 1930s. The interesting thing about turning points is that we rarely know they are turning points at the time. We can wonder what might have happened in Bettine's life if she had continued to be a flier.

Flying

A friend, Bobbie, must have been staying at Kinellan. It

was a cold November day. At a loss for something to do, we decided to go to Hanworth Aviation Club to make enquiries about flying lessons. Bobbie herself was frightened of flying, and never would, but urged me on.

The club was on what is now Heathrow Airport in a large old house in its own grounds. We were directed to a small white hut beside the tarmac. The man in charge gave me the information I needed and then asked if I would like to go on a trial flight. I did not. I had only wanted to find out. The whole thing looked too formidable, I had no intention of flying and tried to get away. But then, one of the instructors appeared and he was so persuasive that I changed my mind.

I was not suitably dressed for the cold in an open cockpit and was only wearing a camelhair coat. Bobbie, although she was much taller than me, took off her coat and put it over mine—it reached the ground. Someone put a helmet on my head. The plane, a de Havilland Gypsy Moth, was a dual control, the instructor in the front cockpit, the pupil in the back one. I was feeling anything but happy. Llewellyn, the instructor, led me to the aeroplane. The only instruction I had was when he said, 'Done any riding? It's a bit the same, a question of hands.'

There was a problem. The plane was high off the ground and there was no means of my reaching it. So he gave me a leg-up. It is one thing on a horse to arrive in the saddle, but in two coats it is not a simple thing to land in a cockpit. I made a most humiliating entry into my new career, landing upside down, head on the floor. Mechanics and other people had to come over and untangle me and prop me right way up.

It was freezing cold with no shelter. Our only means of communication was through the headphones. The control stick was dual—when one moved, the other did.

Llewellyn demonstrated that if you pushed forward the plane went down; pulled it back, it came up. I wished he wouldn't and wanted only to get back on the ground. He asked me to have a go. When I did, it was like magic. I became part of the sky and the clouds. All my fear went. I suppose it is the same feeling as sailing.

So I learnt. It was some time before I was allowed to go solo, but when I did, I always had a feeling of peace somehow. The cares of the world were down there and I was detached from them.

A certain number of solo hours were necessary to qualify for a beginners' A licence, which I did. Then practice was necessary, and I was told what to practise. One day, a new instructor was in charge. There was also another man there who overheard our conversation. I asked the instructor what I should do and he seemed doubtful, so I jokingly suggested a loop-the-loop. I had done this once with the instructor. He agreed, rather to my surprise. I took off, reached the necessary height, but when it came to making the loop, pulled out. I did this a few times, then landed.

The stranger met me and said he had been watching my antics in the sky but had missed the moment when I made the loop. I confessed that I hadn't made one, because when the time came, I was frightened. He asked me how many solo hours I had done. It was about three, I think. He said, 'Thank God that at least you had the sense to be frightened. No-one should even attempt a loop until they have had at least 100 hours.'

He was an aerial photographer and had been on the look-out for someone to fly the plane for him. He took over from my instructor, and later accompanied me on my first cross-country flight. It was a mock air raid, a competition to land at another flying club without being spotted. Sixty people took part, only five got through—two were women. I was one. It made headlines in the Sunday paper—'Women's success!' The aerial photographer wanted me to go into business with him, which would have required more training in navigation and engineering.

I would fly the plane for him and I could have done that. But I went to Austria for a few weeks skiing and met an Australian who urged me to go to Australia. I did, and married him. So ended a career in the sky, which apparently I would have succeeded in, as I was told I had the 'flair' or 'hands' necessary.

Turn to the next workshop for more ideas on how to make an interesting story out of your life.

8
Workshop V: Inventing the story

I am now going upstairs to invent the story of
my life.

Russell Baker

STORY, OR NARRATIVE, is probably the
oldest structure in the human world. Even as the first
people developed speech they began telling stories. They
crouched in the firelight, forgetting the dangerous night
as they listened to the stories of their lives. Perhaps they
listened to the wisest of them tell how the moon came
to be in the sky and why the seasons changed in a
rhythmic way. They would have spoken to each other
softly, persistently, keeping the unknown night from
invading their souls with fear.

Stories are conveyed in art, music and dance as well
as through words. People in all cultures at all times have
used story to make sense of their lives. In fact, the
essential quality of a story is that it joins events together
and thereby gives them meaning.

'Making a good story out of it' is one way of organising the material of your life. In Workshop IV I suggested other ways you might want to use. Each way involves storytelling, of course, but if you feel your life really has a distinct storyline, then you may want to develop the 'story' aspect of it. If the events of your life appear more random, one of the other structures may be more useful.

We all have a story in our minds about what our life means. In his book *The Man Who Mistook His Wife for a Hat* (Duckworth, 1985), Dr Oliver Sacks writes, 'We have, each of us, a life story, an inner narrative—whose continuity, whose sense, *is* our lives. It might be said that each of us constructs and lives a "narrative" and that this is our identity.' This is another way of saying our stories create us.

This inner story tries to make sense of what happens to us and, in some instances, can even create what happens to us. We depend on the continuity of the inner story for our sense of meaning and direction in life. The Buddhist monk Chogyam Trungpa, in *The Myth of Freedom* (Shambhala, 1976), says this continuity is an illusion that the ego generates to avoid facing impermanence. He calls the inner story 'internal gossip'. I suspect he is absolutely right, but I for one am not ready to give up my 'internal gossip'.

If you, like me, are not yet prepared to live entirely in the moment without an inner story, you can use that story to help you structure the writing of your life. It can help you, most importantly, with the problem of what to put in and what to leave out.

'How do I know what to put in and what to leave

out? So much has happened in my life, how do I decide what to use?' These are the questions most often asked by life story writers. The answer can lie in finding the central plot of your inner story, the central storyline around which events seem to happen.

Of course, your life story will almost certainly have more than one storyline. The stories of our lives are usually more complex than that of any novel. Still, you may find there is one central organising idea around which the rest will form. In *A Fortunate Life* (Fremantle Arts Centre Press, 1981), Albert Facey organises his material around the central idea of overcoming hardship.

Ask yourself what is the heart of the story that you want to tell. What is your story about? Is it primarily about a country childhood? Is it about your relationships with your family? Is it about the overcoming of hardship? Is it about the search for your own identity and role in life? Is it about the discovery of your hidden or obscured past?

You may not know the answers to these questions until you are halfway through writing your life story, or until you have finished a first draft—which is why I suggest that you start writing first and see what structure emerges from your material.

'Structure emerging from your material' is one of those phrases writers use which sound terribly vague. It sounds like some kind of bony construction sticking out through the soft folds of your words that you are supposed to be able to see. Indeed, it is like that, although not so obvious. Letting structure emerge is a matter of knowing what to look for.

Look for events or relationships that are repeated.

Look for a pattern of events that resembles the patterns in myths or fairytales that you know. Look, in your own life, for the unfolding of stories that remind you of novels you have read. Your life may be like a mystery, even a romance or a thriller!

When you have recognised these story patterns, you can rearrange your material to emphasise them, and write about them in more detail. If, for example, a description of your daily life at school does not add to your central story—your relationship to your parents—look at it again to see if you can make it more relevant, or leave it out. Of course, if you see the central story from the beginning you will be able to arrange the elements of your life with a particular order and emphasis in mind which can then be refined in rewriting or editing.

When the American columnist Russell Baker was writing his life story, *Growing Up* (Congdon & Weed, 1982), he saw that he had made a mess of his first attempt because he did not realise what it was really about. He had not understood what the real story was. When he realised it was about a strong woman (his mother) and a weak man (himself), he was able to write a wonderful life story. Finding the story helped him to shape his material; to know what to concentrate on in detail and what to leave out as irrelevant. It helped him 'invent the story of his life'.

Particular periods

Some of you may want to write not about your whole life, but about a particular episode. Many powerful life stories have concentrated on a sojourn in a foreign country, a struggle with a life-threatening illness, the loss of a child—any episode that has had an overpowering impact. In such cases your storyline will be obvious. It will be contained by a particular time and a particular issue, but you still have to decide how to plot it. The same story can be plotted in all kinds of different ways. By plot I mean the order and emphasis given to the story. You can start the story in any number of places and tell it in any order, and you can emphasise different aspects of it by going into greater detail.

Some ways of plotting that you could try are:

- Start with a lead-up to the climax, cut back to the beginning and show how events led to this situation, then write the climax and the aftermath.
- Start with a significant early episode and move forward chronologically.
- Start with a mystery or puzzle which is then unfolded by cutting back and forward in time.
- 'Plait' three or four different stories in and out of each other by telling part of one and then another and so on, coming back to each story in turn.
- Use 'flashbacks' to explore the roots of the particular episode you are writing about.

These techniques can be used for plotting general life stories as well as stories focusing on particular episodes, though they may be more easily applied to the latter. Don't try to force a plot on a loose collection of events. It may lead to distortion and awkwardness in your writing.

Different backgrounds

A cultural background different from the mainstream can

often help define the way people feel about themselves. In Australia, the dominant culture is still Anglo-Irish, and if you are from another background your sense of difference can be part of your identity. Many life stories have been written exploring the idea of difference. *My Place*, by Sally Morgan (Fremantle Arts Centre Press, 1987), and *Ruby Don't Take Your Love To Town*, by Ruby Langford (Penguin, 1988), both look at being Aboriginal in white Australia. Andrew Riemer, in *Inside Outside* (Angus & Robertson, 1992), explores the feeling of being an outsider from Eastern Europe in 1940s Australia.

If your identity has been formed to some extent by the fact that your cultural background has not been mainstream, you could try using that as the central organising idea of your story.

Plots of fiction

The plots of fiction can be helpful when you are planning the structure of your life story. I suspect that we may act out certain 'stories' in our lives because those stories have been imprinted in our minds from the books we have read. As a child, I didn't feel anything in my life was real unless it was like something that had happened in a book. I needed my life to resemble fiction to be convinced it was real. That is probably still the case.

Even if you have not lived out stories from fiction in your life (perhaps I am a severe case!), you may have noticed elements of a particular fictional plot in your story. Would your life make a good thriller? An adventure yarn? A mystery? A treasure hunt? A detective story? You can use these story shapes to fashion your own story. If your story is about searching out the hidden truth of your origins, for example, emphasise the detective work you have done.

Again, do not force these structures on your writing. Only use them if the material of your life lends itself to the structures of fiction.

No story?

What if there is no particular story to your life? What if it seems to be simply a collection of random events? Don't worry. As I outlined in Workshop IV, there are many other ways to organise your material. And however you organise it, you will still tell lots of stories.

Perhaps the whole idea of life having a plot is a fiction. I don't mean to imply that life is meaningless and completely random, only to suggest that seeing our life as a story may be a human way of managing the unknown, the darkness at both ends of our lives. As we need food and warmth, so do we need the stories of our lives.

READING

Moon and Rainbow

After the war I got a job on a cattle station just below the Gulf. The owner of that station was a good boss and I had worked for him for a while during the war. I started just before the end of the wet, when the country was still wet and boggy, with water lying everywhere. I didn't know at the time but the Boss had decided to catch his neighbours napping by making a clean sweep of all the calves and cleanskins on their properties while they were still sitting on their verandahs waiting for the country to dry out.

There were five Aborigines, with a white cook and head stockman, in the camp. We all had two horses each and a couple of extra packhorses when we set off to follow a big watercourse away from the homestead. Just before we came to the boundary fence we went into the bed of the river and rode along through shallow water. The head stockman had wirecutters to deal with the fence—already mended in several places after having been broken by wet season floods.

We put out a scout on each side of the river to ride far and wide to make sure there was no-one about. For several days we then mustered along the river and its creeks until we had more than a hundred head of cleanskins, most of them only calves. I knew now we were not just being helpful to the neighbours—but were doing what is known as poddy-dodging and cattle-duffing.

Beef for our camp came from the best branded bullocks, or a nice fat young cow—the sort of beef you don't kill on the home station. Shooting a branded beast is risky work. The brand is proof of ownership and it is wise to get rid of this quickly in case the owner should come riding along to enquire about the shooting.

My mate Billy was butcher for our camp. He was a dead shot even from horseback. As soon as he had selected and shot a fat beast he would gallop up, jump off and cut the brand and ears off with his knife. He would then get a stick and poke this evidence of ownership up the behind of the animal as far as possible. No white man would ever think of searching there. This was far safer than burying it or putting it in a hollow tree. Billy would then slit the hide down the back and peel it off one side. We used to take all the meat off one side, then turn the hide back and turn the beast over to leave the untouched side upwards. Two or three days later—after the crows, dingoes and wild pigs had had their share—you couldn't tell that the beast hadn't died a natural death.

When we had cleaned out that part of the country we drove our small herd back along the riverbed and mended the fence again. We had been careful to leave no trace of our camps and the last showers of the wet season soon washed away our tracks. After raids on two more neighbouring stations our boss was richer by about 500 head. The neighbours must have thought the dingoes were bad that year.

This is an extract from *Moon and Rainbow: The Autobiography of an Aboriginal,* by Dick Roughsey (Reed Books, 1971). As the subtitle indicates, the author has shaped his life story around the fact of being Aboriginal. He has tied the various adventures of his life together under the overarching theme of being Aboriginal in a country dominated by white Australians. Although this extract is told in a straightforward way, there is oblique irony in the fact that he is with a group of white men who are doing what thousands of Aborigines have been killed for—stealing stock. This subtly underlines the central thread of his story, which is his experience of being part of two cultures.

WRITING EXERCISES

1 Plots of fiction

Write an opening page for your life story as if it were a mystery or adventure or thriller, or any other genre that seems appropriate. Everything you write must be true, but use the structures that your chosen genre typically uses. For example, if you decide to write a mystery opening, start with an unexplained event that arouses curiosity, or if you decide on action–adventure, begin by plunging into the action.

2 Threads

Think of an early memory. Has the event or person in the memory continued to be important to you? Write about the memory and then trace how it has recurred throughout your life. This is a longer exercise and may take a couple of hours to do.

3 Traditional story

Imagine your life was written by a novelist. (Perhaps you feel it has been!) Try to plot your life along the lines of a traditional novel, with an introduction—a building of the action—a climax—a denouement. Write headings for events in your life and order them so they fit into these divisions. If they fit comfortably you may find you can write your life as a kind of novel.

4 Reviewer

Imagine you are a reviewer who has just received and read a copy of your life story. As the reviewer, write a short outline of the plot and the concerns of the book. Start with 'This is the story of (your name), who . . .' This is a difficult exercise because it requires you to form an overview of what you intend doing. The discipline of doing this can result in a summary of the story of your book.

Detaching yourself by writing as if you were someone else looking on from the outside can release mental blocks and let you see clearly what the story is. By the way, as the reviewer, you loved the book, so make sure you give it an enthusiastic review!

LIFE STORY WRITERS

Rosemary P. wrote this intriguing beginning for her life story as a response to the first exercise. She had written other beginnings, but this one caught my interest because of the unanswered questions.

A Soul Seeking Liberation
'Come on, kneel down in front of me.'

I did as I was asked and bowed my head towards my old friend.

In front of him, that is, between us, was a bucket of hot water, and in his hand he brandished a safety razor.

'I'll just lather you up first.'

I stayed motionless, fear and joy at the same time filling my heart.

John began to gently massage my head with soap and water and once he had a good lather he began to shave.

'Right, that's done! You can go and look in the mirror now.'

I tentatively put my hand to my head and was astonished to feel the smoothness.

This second, longer piece, by Sue O., began as a response to the second exercise. It is interesting the way the memory of the train becomes a thread connecting many memories together. The memory is also symbolic of a life of journeys and adventures.

Trains
I can still smell the warm, acrid smoke of the steam

trains. I am a small, skinny child again, gasping and laughing in an enveloping cloud as the train passes under the overhead bridge and chugs to destinations unknown. The train leaves me standing alone on the bridge and sensing, even then, that this noisy friend might offer a journey to freedom.

Trains have woven a thread through my life since those early childhood days and any train trip can unravel a string of memories. Memories of living by the railway near Faulconbridge station; memories of our old rented timber house in Sir Henry Parkes Parade, and of dark rooms and sunny verandahs, yellow buttercups, tall gums and wattles, and cubby houses, and windows rattling in the night as the steam trains passed through the town.

There are also memories of fear. Fear of a grandfather who lived in a sunless house at the edge of Sir Henry Parkes cemetery. And there are memories of a grandmother warming herself on a bench in the cemetery, a newspaper over her face, and of two young boys who ran off in terror thinking she was the ghost of Sir Henry Parkes.

Like many families after the war, we were fairly poor, so travelling anywhere was a rare occurrence. The first steam train trip I clearly remember was to Leura to see the Queen. We stood for hours in The Mall to receive a brief disappointing wave before catching the train back down the mountains.

Once a year, our family did manage to go on holidays. We would catch the train to Central, then go by bus to Bungan Beach to stay in an old wooden army hut, acquired by my reverend grandfather after the Second World War, and placed on now-prime land overlooking the beach. I loved those holidays at Bungan with the huge sandhills, the surf, the rock pools, the 'castle' on Bungan Head, and the film star pin-ups on the padre's ex-army-hut walls. These holidays were the start of my yearning to wander, and holidays and travel have been the special times of my life ever since.

I became a regular train traveller in my teenage years. By this time we had moved to the other side of Faulconbridge, away from the train line. This move necessitated a half-hour walk to the station, as our family did not ever own a car. I enjoyed the steam train travel to Katoomba High School in the old box carriages which provided cosy cubby houses for parties and other prohibited behaviour. When electric trains replaced the steam trains, our journey was quicker but some of the excitement disappeared from our days. Thoughts of teenage years bring back memories of the train line on fire at Leura in devastating bush fires in 1957, and memories of talking or fighting with friends on the platform, and of passionate after-dark embraces in the waiting room at Faulconbridge station.

One of my most memorable steam train trips was to Bathurst at Easter time to attend a Presbyterian Fellowship camp. I remember the train snaking through the moonlit whispering grassland and the comforting chug of the engine and the smell of coal smoke. The impression of the journey stayed with me long after the influence of religious instruction had worn off.

Other special wanderings followed. It was a train that took me away from home and office work to Goulburn, where I went to work as a mother's help on a sheep station at Braidwood. In the 1960s, when cars were not so common amongst young people, it was trains which transported me to many of my first bush walks, instilling a love of adventure. Later there were longer trips to Melbourne by train and ferry to Tasmania or back across the Nullarbor from Perth.

Fifteen years ago a very special train journey occurred. I boarded at Hornsby with my husband, Ian, who was holding a baby basket. The other passengers were horrified when he stuffed the basket up onto the luggage rack—until they realised it did not, after all, contain a baby. It was a strange, exciting trip. I felt as though I were going on holidays and could not quite believe I was on my way to instant motherhood. At 5 a.m., after sitting up all night, we alighted at Coffs Harbour, where we caught a taxi to the hospital for our first look at smiling, dark-eyed, eight-week-old Kylie Melissa. Flying home to Sydney later that day with this beautiful, terrifying bundle of responsibility was an overwhelming experience.

My life has changed a great deal since that memorable day and most of my recent travelling has been by car, plane, or square-rigged ship. However, ten years ago I moved back to my beloved Blue Mountains and once again have an association with commuter train travel. Train travel up and down the mountains at present is often fraught with frustration, which drives commuters to write letters to the paper with headings like 'Murder on the Springwood Express'. But I still enjoy an occasional train ride to Sydney, and the sight of a steam train, or any train, evokes in me a wealth of memories and a tug of excitement and expectation.

Somewhere deep inside me there is a small, skinny girl, smelling the coal smoke and dreaming of adventure and freedom.

Turn to the next workshop for discussion and exercises on the topic of style—the crucial question of how to write the material you have gathered.

9

Workshop VI:
A matter of style

Style takes its final shape more from attitudes of mind than from principles of composition.

W. Strunk and E.B. White

STYLE IS A curious thing. Some days, even when I am staying at home, I try on a couple of outfits before I feel comfortable. I don't think it's vanity—I am not so concerned with the way I look as with whether I feel 'right' in my clothes: whether the way I appear relates to the way I am. This relationship is a matter of style.

Some people think style is only to do with appearances. 'All style and no substance' is a common criticism which implies that style is all on the surface. But style is not simply the 'look' of a person; it is, to a certain extent, an expression of that person's feelings and attitudes. Even people who pull on the nearest shirt and trousers are expressing an attitude—perhaps that they are no-nonsense people, or that for them, appearances don't count.

On the other hand, a too-quick reading of style can be misleading. A few months ago, I was on a train late at night when a teenager with a black Megadeth T-shirt and a worryingly shaved head came into the otherwise empty carriage. I made immediate judgments about his intelligence, character, personal habits, family background and life potential, all based on a split-second appraisal of his style. None of my judgments was generous, and none of them contributed to my feelings of security. Then he sat down and pulled out a copy of Jane Austen's *Pride and Prejudice* and started to read. I suddenly felt more relaxed.

I had misread his style. As Jane Austen knew, judgments based on first impressions can be wrong. Still, style is part of, and affects, content. There can be no content without style of some kind. Your personal style will inevitably say something about your attitudes, just as your style of writing will say something about your attitudes to your life.

Writing style, like dress style, is made up of a number of different elements. Voice, point of view, tone, tense, choice of words and sentence structure, even content, all go towards making up a particular style. They do not work separately but are inextricably woven together. To me, the single most important stylistic element is voice.

Voice

Voice is the sound of the author 'speaking' to the reader. It is how you 'sound' as the person telling the story, the author writing the book. It is made up of all the other aspects of style.

Your voice is constructed by all your experiences and

everything you have heard and read, but it is still uniquely your own. Nevertheless, it is not always simple to reconstruct it on the page. All the books you have read can get in the way and influence you to write in the voice of writers you admire. If you try to write in a particular 'literary' voice, you may end up sounding as if the books you've read are stuck in your throat. Try to write the way you speak and your writing voice, with practice, will come through clear and true.

Tone

Tone is the aspect of voice which shows the writer's attitude to the experiences they are writing about. We often hear the remark, 'It wasn't what she said, it was her tone of voice'. Your attitude, or tone, may be philosophic, ironic, sardonic, light-hearted, intense, mocking, serious, familiar, detached, tentative, authoritative—or a mixture of all of the above.

Your tone of voice when you speak usually varies according to the situation. I suggest that the tone you use with a trusted friend is a good one to use when writing your life story. You are not straining to impress, but neither do you impose; nor are you too familiar. It is *your* life story. Write it with your own attitude towards it; with the voice you have inside you.

Point of view

If voice is 'who's speaking', point of view is 'who's looking'. Where you look from determines what you see. If you are on top of a mountain, people look small; if you are a small child, a table looks huge.

In writing, point of view is not just a matter of

111

physical place; you also have a psychological point of view which is influenced by your age, sex, social class, nationality and life experience. You see events, people, yourself, from a unique point of view.

When writing your own life story, you are writing from your own point of view and so will generally use what is referred to as the first person (I, we). However, if you are getting tired of writing 'I' all the time, you can vary it by writing about yourself in the third person (he, she, they), as if you were looking at your life from the outside. This can be a good antidote if you feel you are becoming self-indulgent and is also useful if you are finding a particular incident too embarrassing or too painful to write. You can shift back and forth between first and third person, or even write the whole of your life story in the third person. Try writing certain sections in the third person and see what happens.

When writing your life story, your point of view will also be influenced by your distance in time from events. Clearly, your attitude to people and events shifts over time. Should you, for example, write about the time your father hit you with a strap from your point of view then, frightened and confused, or from your point of view now, understanding the stress he was under because of losing his job? Try writing from both viewpoints, and write about the shift in your perspective on the event.

You may like to write about some events directly from the point of view of the child you were. Often you will find yourself falling naturally into a child's point of view when you write about childhood incidents. This can give a freshness and a lovely childlike quality to your writing. A constant adult re-evaluation can distract from the feeling of revelation that pervades the child's world. Your point of view of incidents will not necessarily be the same as that of others who were there at the same time. Who is to say whose view is correct? You are the only person looking at your life from your particular vantage point, and you are free to say what you can see from there.

Still, it can be interesting to write about an event from someone else's point of view. This can be especially useful where there has been conflict. Even if you don't use the result in your life story, it might help resolve, or at least illuminate, a difficult area so that you can write about it more freely.

Tense

Tense, in the grammatical sense, means whether you write about events as if they have happened in the past, are happening in the present, or will happen in the future. Most fiction and life story writing is in the past tense. Generally, a piece of writing is more coherent if it remains in the same tense throughout.

Choosing tense can become a problem for life story writers. You will probably find it easiest to write in the past tense, but every now and then something may seem so immediate to you, even now, that you will want to write about it in the present tense. Go ahead—you can break the general rule. Writing in the present tense can make events very vivid. Remember, though, don't slip backwards and forwards in tense to no purpose, as it becomes confusing to the reader. If you change tense, do it for a reason and do it in a regular, consistent way.

Words and sentences

Many grammar and style books have been written about choosing the correct word and structuring sentences properly. All I will add to them is: use the words and sentences you feel comfortable with. I'm not saying that grammar and sentence structure don't matter; they are all-important, the precision tools of a writer's trade. I am saying that you shouldn't let anxiety about correct usage stop you from writing your life story.

Look to the way you picture things in your mind. Use your own everyday words and your own everyday sentences. If you feel your grammar is muddled you can always ask someone else to sort it out for you when you are finished. As you write you will become more confident and then you can experiment with different ways of expressing yourself.

Words and sentences can be thought of as a magician's props. As a magician appears to create a dove, you can create your life in words. We often feel someone we have read about is just as real as someone we know, even though we have only met them in words. You don't have to be a master magician, but as you continue with your writing you will become more and more skilful at using words to recreate your life on the page.

Content

Content itself is part of style. What in your life you choose to write about is an element of your style. You may decide to write about only the amusing and entertaining events of your life—that is your style. It may be your style to be reserved and leave out some of the more passionate details. These choices about content are all part of your style as a writer.

Your writing style will probably relate to your personal style, your characteristic way of going about things. If you are generally informal in your personal style, your writing is likely to have a similar style. If you are crisp and well-organised in your personal style, your writing will probably be likewise.

Style is cultivated by everything we see and read but it is also an individual characteristic. Don't be concerned with choosing a style but write what you think and feel and your style will become apparent. Being unsure at first, you will probably wobble, becoming too flowery at times, or too stiff, or too vague. Keep writing. Later, as your style develops, you can go back and edit. You may admire a particular writer's style and want to emulate it. While it is generally a useful learning technique to copy the work of someone you admire, in writing your life story, it's especially important that you find and develop your own style. *Write your own story in your own way.*

READING

The Watcher on the Cast-Iron Balcony

In a half-century of living I have seen two corpses, two only. I do not know if this is conventional or unconventional for an Australian of my age.

The first corpse is that of a woman of forty. I see its locked and denying face through a lens of tears, and hear, beyond the useless hullaballoo of my debut in grief, its unbelievable silence prophesying unbelievable silence for me. It is not until twenty-eight years later that I see, through eyes this time dry and polished as glass, my second corpse, which is that of a seventy-three-year-old man. Tears? No tears, not any, none at all. The silence of this corpse is as credible as my own silence is to be, and no excuse for not lighting another cigarette. I light it, tearless, while the bereaved others scatter their anguish in laments like handbills. I am tearless because twenty-eight years have taught me that it is not the dead one should weep for but the living.

Once upon a time, it seems, but in reality on or about the day King Edward VII died, these two corpses have been young, agile and lustful enough to mortise themselves together to make me. Since the dead wear no ears that hear and have no tongues to inform, there can now be no answer, should the question be asked, as to where the mating takes place, how zestfully or grotesquely, under which ceiling, on which kapok mattress—no answer anywhere, ever.

In time, the woman, Mother, is six months large with me, and Dr Crippen is hanged. In time, and missing Edwardian babyhood by nine months, I am born. I am born a good boy, good but not innocent, this two-sided endowment laying me wide open to assaults of evil not only from without but also from within. I am a Thursday's child with far to go, brought forth under the sign of Aquarius, and with a cleft palate. This is skilfully sewn up. In which hospital? When I am how few months old? By whom now dead or nearing death? No-one, I think, no-one living now knows. Thus secretly mended, and secretly carrying, as it were, my first lie tattooed on the roof of the mouth which is to sound out so many later lies, I grow. I am exactly one week old when the first aeroplane ever to do so flies over my birthplace. On aesthetic grounds or for superstitious reasons I am unvaccinated; I am superstitiously and fashionably uncircumcised, plump, blue-eyed and white-haired. I have a silver rattle, Hindu, in the shape of a rococo elephant hung on a bone ring. I crawl. The *Titanic* sinks. I stand. The Archduke is assassinated at Sarajevo, and I walk at last into my own memories.

The opening of *The Watcher on the Cast-Iron Balcony*, by Hal Porter (Faber & Faber, 1963), is very clever and stylish. Porter was already an experienced writer when he began this first book of his autobiography, so his characteristic sardonic voice is strong and clear. His point of view is detached and his use of language is extraordinarily playful, with lots of puns and conceits and unusual juxtapositions. At the same time his writing is full of insights and close observations of himself and others. If you appreciate a witty and intelligent style, you will enjoy the three books of Porter's autobiography.

WRITING EXERCISES

1 *Another view*

Take an incident from your childhood or teenage years and write about it in the first person but from the point of view of someone else who was there at the time. In effect you will be writing about yourself from someone else's point of view. Try this from any number of other people's points of view—a parent, a brother or sister, a teacher, a friend, an enemy. See if your writing style changes when you are writing from someone else's viewpoint. You may not use the results of this exercise in your life story, but it is a great way to see how point of view can influence style, and it is a good way of gaining insight into yourself and others.

2 First job—third person

A timed exercise—30 minutes. Write about your first job or, if you have come to Australia from overseas, your first job in Australia. Write about your experience from your point of view as if you were telling it to a friend, i.e. write what you really think, not what you think other people want to hear. Try to write in the voice which is characteristically yours, so that people who know you can read it and say 'That sounds like you.'

3 A style sharpener

Write about an important person in your life without telling anything about them. How? Show them in action and in conversation. Don't write that they were kind or mean or gentle or violent, *show* them acting that way and write dialogue that lets readers see for themselves what kind of person they were. This will make your writing more lively. The next chapter will have more discussion and exercises on bringing your writing to life.

4 More style sharpeners

Write about an important person in your life or an important event, perhaps a turning point in your life. Now cross out every single adjective. Read through what you have written and notice how the style has changed. Now try writing about another person, from the beginning using no adjectives at all. This is difficult to do, as most of us were taught at school to use lots of descriptive words, but it is very useful, especially if you think your style is a bit flowery or purple. Too many adjectives can clutter and weigh down your writing, so that your readers end up seeing only adjectives instead of what you want them to see. You don't have to drop adjectives forever, but these exercises are an excellent way to make your writing clearer and sharper.

LIFE STORY WRITERS

Eleanor C.'s story is a response to Exercises 1 and 3 combined. She wrote this incident in the first person from her husband's point of view, and she used dialogue and action to convey something of his character.

Footloose

I was striding across the huge concrete apron outside the construction site when my foot and I parted company. The poor bulldozer driver, piling up soil in the beautification strip beyond, almost fell off his machine.

'Don't just sit there,' I yelled. 'Would you go inside and get the painter.'

He hesitated.

'Any painter—they are working in there somewhere.'

The man slowly disappeared into the building, shaking his head in disbelief. I wobbled helplessly on a crippled wooden ankle.

'Damn the thing!' I knew I should have got it fixed weeks ago when it first started to swivel around, and old ladies and young men looked in amazement as I bent to twist it back to front. But this was no joke. Here I was, stuck like a shag on a rock in a sea of concrete.

Danny, my charge-hand, came out, his face

contorting with sympathy, humour and a hint of malice. It wasn't often you had your boss at your mercy.

'God!' he exclaimed.

'Don't stand there.' I fished in my pocket for the keys, almost overbalancing in the attempt.

'Here, get the ute, it's over there.' I pointed to a huddle of cars and utilities parked on the tamped-down earth beyond the concrete and partly finished landscaping.

Later on I would laugh about this, but now I was overwhelmed with embarrassment and helplessness.

Danny gave me a hand into the driver's seat. I was still capable of driving; by law the vehicle was modified to ensure that. On arrival at the Repatriation Limb Factory I sent Danny to borrow crutches so I could get inside. I tolerated a lecture from the powers that be, left my leg for repairs, and headed off to drop Danny at the job and return home to my spare leg in the wardrobe.

Wilson C. wrote the following piece about his first job in Australia after he arrived here from the Philippines with his wife and three children. He writes with his characteristic sharp observation and skeptical, wry voice.

What's on the Road Ahead

Three months ago the decision was simple—well, not so simple. Starting a new life in Australia as a lowly paid factory worker with a family of five to depend on that pay, and after only 48 hours in the country, was not necessarily an act of desperation. I could easily have opted for unemployment benefits, considerably higher than the factory job paid, while looking for something more appropriate to my training and experience. But I did not want to lose a moment to find out, in order to find myself in relation to the land of OZ, whether Australia was the proud and clever country that its politicians say it is.

The factory, the heart and soul of the industrial religion, was my second choice as a first step in the journey ahead. I wanted a job with the garbage collection department—an almost impossible aim, being new and non-union and from the wrong part of the globe. It would have been perfect to discover the biggest former penal colony in the world through its backside.

My decision was a conscious act of commitment to a new way of life. I am a migrant, an Oriental from a non-English-speaking background. The young fair woman at the Commonwealth Employment Office asked me if I could speak English. I said yes. She looked at my job qualifications as we talked. She was a nice person. But slowly I began to understand from her other 'employment officer' person, that by some weird logic of the system my extensive university studies and teaching experience were nothing, nothing more than figments of my imagination. Why? Simple, because they were obtained from a non-English-speaking background and therefore non-existent, or at most, inferior.

She apologised. Equal employment opportunity is government policy and there is no racial discrimination in Australia. 'But what can I do? That is the rule. By the way, there is a factory demand for a general hand at Kirrawee, if you are interested.' We stared at each other for a moment. We both laughed. She arranged an interview for me with the factory. I got the job on the spot.

A master's degree in philosophy, ten years teaching in the academy, and being 46 years old, are not exactly the right training for a factory peon. The first month was hell. But I soon became intimate with every fibre in my body and sharpened my knowledge of human anatomy.

Nightly, I could name the several hundred muscles and bones in my body by the same number of aches and pains. By the second month I was fully enjoying the job.

The factory building was a formless and ugly prefabricated structure, like all the plants sprouting like pimples around Sydney. Inside was dusty, noisy and unhealthy: freezing in winter and boiling hot in summer. The name of the game was profit, fuelled by cheap migrant labour. The company produced speakers for stereos and public sound systems.

In two months I was a good factory hand. I could assemble the components with my eyes closed, spray paint the wooden castings, pack them into cardboard boxes and load them onto big trucks while humming 'Waltzing Matilda' and not miss a beat.

It was by the end of the third month that I paid more attention to what I was handling. As I worked on the assembly line I noticed disturbing signs of the state of the Australian dream. The woofers and tweeters were made in Taiwan, the amplifiers made in Hong Kong, the screws and drivers made in the People's Republic of China, and the big plant machines bore instructions in Nippongo. Only the wood and the labour were Australian. It dawned slowly on my unbelieving mind that the 'clever' country was a myth. Australia was going down the Argentinian road, a fetcher of water and a hewer of wood for the industrialised nations of Asia. The signs are there in that factory.

It was Friday. It was payday, always my favourite day these last three months. I drew my pay. I walked leisurely from the factory through the main street of Kirrawee, past the ugly factories, the shops pregnant with goods, the banks and their sharp-eyed moneylenders, the bottle shop doing its usual Friday double time, the silent apartment houses, the concrete steps down to the railway station. It then occurred to me that this was the last time I would walk this familiar road. I had made up my mind that moment that there was nothing more to learn in the factory.

Turn to the next workshop for ideas on how to make your writing more lively and interesting.

10
Workshop VII: Bringing it to life—drama

All the world's a stage,
And all the men and women merely players

William Shakespeare

'BRING IT TO life' is a mysterious piece of advice often directed at writers. It seems to assume that writers have the power of the gods to give life. People even remark that a writer they admire 'breathes life into his characters'. The mysterious part is that the assumption is correct. In a sense, writers do give life to characters and to their surroundings. A fiction writer creates characters, gives them traits and actions and speech. Life story writers do not create characters, but they can bestow life by giving the people they know actions and speech on the page. They make events come alive by the way they write about them.

The way to bring your writing to life can be summed up in E.M. Forster's famous maxim, 'Show, don't tell'. He was a novelist but the advice is just as useful for a life story writer. It sounds good, but what does it mean? We need to tease his succinct motto out a little.

Put another way, 'Show, don't tell' means: do not recount what has happened as if you are telling the story over a cup of tea; show us what happened as if you were acting out the events on a small stage. In other words, dramatise the events and people in your life story.

Perhaps the easiest way to see the difference between showing and telling is to compare two accounts of the same event.

Passage A
While I was in India I stayed at an ashram in a huge shed with hundreds of other Foreign Ladies. I felt lonely and alienated and it made me judge everyone around me in a harsh and nasty way. I read books while the others were out of the shed and pretended to meditate when they were around so they wouldn't question me in broken English. I remember when I went out one morning I was unpleasant to a perfectly innocent American girl because her naive manner and flowery sari irritated me.

Passage B
The chanting stopped suddenly and I knew the others would be returning to the shed in a few minutes. I closed my book, *A Passage to India*—I was always appropriate with my novels—and sat up and crossed my legs in an approximate lotus position. No-one would speak to me if I looked as if I were meditating.

Opening my eyes slightly, I saw the German woman on the next mattress slip out of her sari and begin her yoga in T-shirt and underpants. I was envious of her supple body. My body felt thick, as if the blood had congealed in my veins. I wanted to cry out, to wail and frighten all the Foreign Ladies. Instead I went to the bathroom, put on some bright red lipstick and went out into the harsh morning.

The grounds were crowded with dusty buses parked in every available space and women untying bundles and children playing. I bumped into a blonde American woman I'd seen in the meal queue.

'What's going on?' The words sounded pinched, as if my throat was closing over.

'A festival of *saddhus*. Isn't it wonderful!' Her scrubbed face beamed. Her beautiful hair was plaited severely down her back and she wore a pale floral sari. I felt pleased with my vicious red mouth.

'Where are the *saddhus*?'

'They are with Swami. They have come from all over India. They wander across the country and their only destination is Truth.'

'So I've heard.' I despised her unquestioning eyes and ecstatic twanging. And her floral sari. At least Indian women wore defiant glorious colours. Westerners shouldn't be allowed to wear saris—they always look so prim.

'And do you think you would like to be a *saddhu*?'

'I'd be anything Swami wanted me to be. I believe he wants me to teach in Hawaii. That's where I'm from. That's where I can do most good for Swami.'

'I suppose so. And the beaches are nice too.' I tried to smile but it didn't work so I walked away abruptly. The American tugged her sari conscientiously around her shoulders.

In the first piece I am telling you how I felt. There is no evidence of this, however, no actions or words, and you may not be convinced or even interested. At any rate, my account would not arouse any emotion or moral response in you because there is nothing in it to remember, nothing to appeal to your senses.

In the second piece you can see and hear the alienation turning to sour criticism. You don't have to be told how I feel, you can see and feel it for yourself. Your senses respond to the sights and the sounds.

Of course, you are not really seeing or hearing anything. It's all the illusion of writing, which makes you feel you have seen and heard and smelt an event which has existed for you only as words on a page. This is the magic of words, that they have the fantastic capacity to create not only events but people whom we respond to as if we knew them ourselves.

Appeal to the senses

The writer gives us this feeling of knowing people we've never met and being at events we've never experienced by appealing to the senses. Or rather, by 'tricking' the mind into believing it is receiving information from the senses. We first know the world through the senses. After that we form ideas about the world and then we philosophise about what the world means. Our sensory experience is primary—if we were deprived of all our senses we could not know the world at all. The 'trick' in writing is to describe your world, your family, your life, so that the mind receives the information as coming from the senses. That is, write the sound, smell, feel, taste, look, of your life.

In this way you can 'show' us your life and the events and the people in it. Instead of just telling us about your beloved grandfather or your teasing uncle, show us. Instead of simply telling us about what happened that day in the schoolyard, let us see and hear what went on. Write the dialogue, write the bell ringing in the background, write the buzz of the flies around a sweaty face.

I can't remember the exact words

You may find that you remember an incident but cannot remember exactly what everyone said. It doesn't matter. Hardly anyone remembers exactly what anyone said. But you can remember the gist of it. That is enough to create the dialogue you need to bring it to life. Approximate what people said, use their characteristic words and phrases. Let them speak.

You may feel uncomfortable putting words into the mouths of your family and friends, knowing that this may not be what they actually said.

You may feel it is a kind of lie to make up someone else's words. The truth is, writing *is* a kind of lie. It pretends to be life, to be flesh and blood and breath; it is an astounding, bald-faced pretence. But sometimes, most times, the truth needs the help of 'let's pretend', of imagination, to be conveyed with any power.

So it doesn't matter if your mother didn't really use those exact words. Write what is likely, write the to and fro of a conversation that never actually occurred, create the living, breathing feel of your family and your times. It will be more truthful, more real, than a flat, factual account of events.

Written conversation

Written conversation is very different from spoken conversation. When you first start writing conversation you may find that it sounds too formal and stiff. This is because writing is structured differently from speech. Hardly anyone speaks in perfect grammar. Speech is looser in structure and contains more fragments, more repetitions, and more 'filling-in' words. In speech, people rarely say anything precisely and they do not recount what they are doing. That is why speech in soapies often sounds false—characters say exactly what they mean and recount large chunks of their activities to move the story along.

To write a spoken conversation effectively, you need to break a lot of the rules of written grammar. Listen to real conversation for a while. Listen to the way you talk. Even tape a conversation if you can ignore the presence of the tape recorder and speak naturally. Then try to write the way people talk. You will find that it is probably too repetitious and perhaps almost incoherent when you try to read it on the page. A halfway point between actual speech and formal grammar, an approximation of speech which sounds real on the page, works best.

When you are writing a conversation, make sure everyone doesn't sound the same. Each person has a different rhythm of speech and uses different words. Vary the lengths of each individual's speeches and use their characteristic words and phrases.

Show everything?

'Show, don't tell' is an absolute piece of advice which you are not meant to follow absolutely. Your life story would be much too long if you dramatised every event in it. Besides, lots of events do not bear dramatising; it would give them a significance they never had in real life.

The idea is to use a mixture of both. Look at any of E.M. Forster's novels to see how he applies his own advice. His writing is always a mixture of telling and showing, a rich tapestry of dialogue, action, description and his own comments.

In your life story you can cover a period of years by telling about it and then dramatise one or two memorable incidents. Or write an account of someone who was important in your life and then show them in conversation and in action to create a more powerful impression of what they were like.

Too much telling can become dull. It is like telling a story in the same voice for hours on end. The audience longs to hear a different voice, to see some action. They probably stop listening and may even doze off. Brighten up your storytelling with dialogue and specific incidents so that your readers, whether your family or the wider world, will want to keep listening to you.

READING

A Fortunate Life

On the morning of the twelfth day I got up at daylight, and looking over towards the new land that had a nice crop growing, I saw about sixty head of cattle grazing. This puzzled me, as we hadn't seen any cattle around other than our own. I chased them away, but I had no sooner got back to the house than they were back again. So after feeding the pigs and fowls, I got Prince in and saddled him, then rode across again to chase the cattle off. This time I took my rifle with me. I thought if I fired a few shots into the air, it would frighten them into not coming back again.

I put Prince into a canter heading straight towards the cattle, and when I considered I was close enough, I fired two quick shots into the air. Wow! I didn't expect what I got. The cattle bolted towards the bush where they had come from and Prince jumped sideways, throwing me heavily onto the ground. Then he bolted back to the stable. My rifle was thrown to the ground and was covered with thick red wet earth.

I picked myself up. I wasn't hurt but felt a little shaken. The cattle had all cleared out—the shots had done the job. I picked up my rifle and was about to walk back to the house, when I heard a man on horseback coming towards me. He rode up to me and said, 'What in the hell do you think you're doing?' I said that I was chasing the cattle off the crop. He replied, 'Who gave you permission to shoot my cattle?' I replied, 'I fired the shots into the air to frighten them off.' He yelled, 'Like hell you did. There's two lying dead over the hill.' I said, 'I couldn't have fired the shots that killed them. I fired into the air, then my horse threw me off.' He came towards me saying, 'You shot them, you little stinker. I'll learn you a lesson.' He started to unwind a large stockwhip. Seeing this, I quickly brought my rifle up to my shoulder and called out, 'Don't come any closer if you want to live.' I must have looked like I meant it because he stopped, turned his horse around and said, 'You will be hearing more of this.' He rode off towards where the cattle had gone.

I walked back to the stable, where Prince was waiting for me. He was frightened and went to run away, so I put the rifle down and went over to him, catching hold of the bridle. He smelt me and became his old quiet self again.

I looked after the sheep and cows and went inside to get some breakfast. While eating my breakfast I wondered how this man could blame me for killing two of his cattle. It was only a few minutes from when I fired the shots until he appeared, and he said that his cattle were dead over the hill. This puzzled me. I felt scared but I was sure that I had fired the shots into the air and away from the cattle. I got the rifle and looked into the magazine—there were still four cartridges left and I remembered that there had been six in it. I hadn't put any more in the rifle.

After a while I was even surer that I hadn't killed the cattle. The only thing I had done wrong was point the rifle at the man and threaten him to warn him. It was the sight of the whip that made me point the rifle at him.

This is part of an incident inscribed in *A Fortunate Life*, by Albert Facey (Fremantle Arts Centre Press, 1981). His life story is one of the most famous ever written in Australia, read by more Australians than any other 20th-century book. It is popular for many reasons but probably most of all because Facey writes with humour and courage about the life of a battler—the archetypal Australian.

It is written in a straightforward way, and he brings incidents such as this one to life by including detailed action and dialogue. Facey probably couldn't remember the exact words the man said to him after seventy years, but he makes it sound right. Time and again, Facey tells us, without blinking an eye, precisely what people said, often at the precise time, and never lets us doubt his memory. If you haven't read *A Fortunate Life*, read it for its lively voice and for the way Facey dramatises incidents so that we can see and hear them.

WRITING EXERCISES

1 Tell and show

There are two parts to this exercise. First, recall an important friendship or love affair. Tell the story of how you first met and got to know each other in no more than half a page. Second, write the same story, this time *showing* how you first met and how your friendship developed, using particular incidents, dialogue, and description. Leave a day or so between doing the two parts of this exercise so you can take a fresh approach in the second part. The second part is likely to be pages longer than the first, even though it deals with the same material.

2 An argument

Think about conflicts you have had with other people. Write the dialogue of one significant argument. It may be with the friend or lover in the first exercise, or it may be an argument with a parent, a child, or a business associate that became a turning point in your life. Try to be as fair as you can in representing each person's point of view. This can be used in your life story as part of a longer sequence about your relationship with the person in question.

3 Collage

Think of something that has happened to you a number of times. It may be holidays at a particular place, or going to school, or visiting your grandmother, or circuses coming to town. Consider your snippets of memories from the many instances of similar events. Then write your memories as if they all happened on the one day. For example, write about a typical day at school using your memories of many different school days. This way, instead of writing generally about recurring events such as school days, you write specifically about a typical day and so bring it to life.

4 Vague memories

Select an incident which you have always remembered even though you can't recall the details. Try to bring it to life by inventing possible details, for example the colour and style of the dress you may have worn, and the conversations you may have held. Think about the location, the weather, what other people were wearing. I don't mean you should write things that are completely imaginary, but that you should use other memories to create a convincing picture. If your husband usually wore his sleeves rolled up, write that his sleeves were rolled up even if you cannot remember noticing his sleeves on that particular day. Write the words of conversations that you know happened, even though you can't actually remember a single phrase. This is a good freeing-up exercise for people who feel they cannot put words into other people's mouths. Try it: you will be delighted with the way a vague memory springs to life, as if it had only been waiting for you to breathe life into it.

LIFE STORY WRITERS

Graham A. wrote a whole chapter about a circus coming

to his small New Zealand village of Putaruru in the 1920s, from his memories of three or four different circuses. It would have been too scrappy if he had written about each one, and combining them in this way gives the 'true' flavour of his boyhood experiences of the circus. I have used an extract from his chapter to illustrate the way he has brought the episode to life by *showing* us the events—especially the elephant waltz!

The Waltzing Elephant

I was lying under the clothes line watching a hawk circling still-winged round and round, round and round, away up in the turquoise sky. Arms spread-eagled, feet bare, I was aware of the scent of the grass, the feel of the sun, the crisp spring air, but I was centred on the hawk.

Behind where I lay was the cowshed and beyond that a paddock where a few cows grazed with old Duke the draught horse and my wonderful roan stock horse, Ginger. She had been a wild horse running on the plains beyond Mamuka, where it was said there was a thoroughbred stallion that had escaped. A friend of Dad's, Mr Krow, had caught her, broken her in and presented her to me. She looked like an Arab and was every bit as lively and willing.

Suddenly, I was aroused from my reveries with the hawk by a thundering of horses' hooves and a tremendous snort. I leapt to my feet to an amazing sight, an almost unbelievable sight—two real live elephants lumbering past the barn towards the cowshed.

Of course, neither Ginger nor I had ever seen such astonishing animals. The effect on her was to send her wild with what seemed to me to be a mixture of fear and indignation. She galloped madly around the paddock, pausing to snort at various vantage points which got further and further away as the elephants got nearer.

I had an advantage. I had always been keen on wild animals and had spent many fascinating hours poring over magazines and books about them, so I did know about elephants. I ran down and, from what was probably considerably more than a safe distance, asked the man who was with them what was happening. He said they were from a circus which had just arrived in the village and which Dad had given permission to water the elephants at the stock trough behind the cowshed.

There was a horse trough in the centre of the village, just over the railway crossing, but if Ginger was any guide, clearly the effect on the local horses of watering elephants there would not have endeared the circus to the villagers. The next move, of course, was helter skelter down the road to see the great tent being erected on a bit of no-man's-land opposite the post office. The next, a breathless request to the parents to be allowed to attend that night's performance. Bless their hearts, this was granted, and soon there I was, tense with excitement, on the front seat facing the ring.

I have vague memories of trapeze artists, performing dogs, jugglers, tumblers, and statuesque, scantily clad ladies standing on the backs of great dappled grey horses cantering around the ring with arched necks and tails flying. But three events I recall very clearly.

The first was a bucking donkey. The ringmaster offered a pound note to any boy who could ride it bareback. A pound seemed a vast sum of money for a small boy to win, but it soon became apparent that the circus owner was not risking his money.

No boy, small or large, could ride that donkey.

Effortlessly and in quick succession it unseated all contenders. Furthermore, this talented animal did not have a bucking strap buckled around its loins as is common in modern day rodeos.

Next, two men wheeled in a heavy, brightly coloured tub and turned it upside down in the middle of the ring. The band struck up a march. On came a beautiful, spangled young lady followed by one of the elephants. On her command, it stepped up onto the tub. The band music changed to a waltz. The elephant swung its right front leg and the opposite back one out to the right in time with the music, then vice versa with the other two legs. At the same time, from between its back legs it lowered an enormous penis, fully as long, I felt, as I was tall, and as thick as the legs of Grandpa's big kitchen table. From it gushed a mighty stream of urine.

Elephants seem to spend their life swaying to and fro, but of course the waltz greatly accentuated this movement. As a result the organ swung in an arc, back and forth across the tub. Every time it crossed the tub, urine splashed in every direction.

If this was part of the performance, it certainly was gripping, but I felt embarrassed for the pretty lady. However, she seemed quite unperturbed, just stepping back out of the splash zone.

After what seemed an age, the torrent ceased. The giant retractable organ disappeared into its recess in the great body—fascinating. But this, it soon became apparent, was only act one. The elephant now began to defecate. Massive dollops of dung descended in waltz time to form an awe-inspiring heap on the ground.

Eventually the waltz ended with a flourish, the lady gave a command, the huge animal stepped down from the tub and followed her with dignity from the ring.

The band played a fanfare, whereupon in rushed a

muscular-looking man, another man with a wheelbarrow and shovel, a clown, and the ringmaster, not necessarily in that order. The ringmaster cracked his whip, the clown turned somersaults, the muscular man removed the tub, the other filled the wheelbarrow and wheeled off the dung. Dee dahh, blared out the band. Most impressive.

The ringmaster was a cruel-looking man with shiny black leggings, riding britches, black cutaway coat, flowing white cravat with a flashy pin, shiny black slicked-down hair and a waxed moustache. In his right hand he carried a stock whip.

The clown wore baggy clothes and his face was made up to look sad with a downturned mouth and doleful eyes. A verbal interchange between him and the ringmaster appeared to develop into an argument, their voices getting louder and louder and the ringmaster becoming more and more threatening until, finally, he stood off and started whipping the clown.

He must have been an expert with the stockwhip which cracked fiercely on the clown's legs, arms, body and even face, or so it seemed to me. The clown cried great sobs of agony, and I bawled and screamed in unison and sympathy, tears streaming down my face—the dawning, perhaps, of my lifelong hatred and fear of violence and cruelty.

Turn to the next workshop for ideas on the other important aspect of bringing your writing to life—fresh and well-observed detail.

11
Workshop VIII: Bringing it to life—detail

We were here; we are human beings; this is how we lived. Let it be known, the earth passed before us. Our details are important. Otherwise, if they are not, we can drop a bomb and it doesn't matter.

Natalie Goldberg

ON A MORNING like any other morning, I walked into the backyard and saw sunlight glowing on an old bench. The bench was sturdy and plain. My tousle-haired son sat there eating his breakfast in the morning light. His arms looked soft on the grey wood, which had stood in the rain and sun for years before he was born.

Later I walked down the hill to the ferry on my way to class. The path led down through a tangle of tree ferns, gum trees and lantana. Underfoot I could feel the damp ground and all around was dappled light, pennies of light shifting and changing on the railing beside the path and on the mosaic of brown and yellow leaves on the steps. In the dim green I saw a red lily. It was still and passionate, the leaves folded away from the flower like broad flat spears.

Once the path reached the bottom of the hill it wound along the edge of the bay until it reached the ferry wharf. As I came to the bay I looked out and saw an old man with a white beard in a white dinghy. The dinghy bobbed up and down on the sparkling waters of the bay as the old man rowed strongly towards shore. The headland behind him was golden sandstone, weathered by wind and sea.

This was a morning fifteen years ago. I have remembered it because, for no known reason, my eyes were wide open. Most days I got up, had breakfast and went to class as a matter of habit. This day, the veil of habit was torn and I saw the fine detail of the world around me. It was as if the world had been made that morning, or my eyes were seeing it for the first time. Habit fell around me again, but I have always remembered that if I take the time to look, there is beauty in any ordinary day.

I don't imagine I'm the only one who lives in a habitual way. A Russian literary critic of the 1920s, Victor Shklovsky, remarked that we, all of us, live most of our lives by habit. He said 'Habitualisation devours work, clothes, furniture, one's wife, and the fear of war'. In other words, habit stops us from actually seeing the objects around us, the people close to us, and even our own emotions. Habit causes 'life to be reckoned as nothing', Shklovsky said, but he went on to argue that the purpose of art was to 'restore the sensation of life; to make one feel things; to make the stone *stony*'.

It is certainly true that 'restoring the sensation of life' is one of the purposes of writing a life story. When people read your story you will want them to feel something of what your life has been like. To remove the veil of habit and restore life, to make the stone *stony,* it is necessary to observe the details of your experience.

To observe accurately you need to become absorbed in your subject. The New Zealand writer Katherine Mansfield said in her journal that she 'became' the thing she was writing about. She observed it, became absorbed in it, until she felt she was the thing itself. Everything she wrote gave the 'sensation of life' because of her absorbed awareness of the details.

This kind of awareness is the natural gift of childhood. A child is seeing the world for the first time. Sand underfoot is hot, the smell of crushed gum leaves is pungent, the earth under the geraniums by the back step is damp and cool. The world is new and the child absorbs every detail.

In Workshop I, I set exercises about early childhood, not so much because childhood comes first, but because of the quality of a child's awareness of the world. Almost everyone writes well about their childhood because, as they return to it in memory, they see and hear as a child once more. They write what they see with their child's awareness, absorbed in the world around them, and so write with clear, absorbing detail.

The question is, how can you bring those childhood eyes into later periods of your life and into the present? Doing this doesn't mean you should look innocently at the world—that is impossible; nor should you look naively—that would be foolish. It does mean 'staying awake', as Buddhist teaching puts it, in your way of seeing the world. Put habit aside and be awake to your life and to the world around you.

When you write about any period, try to remember the individual details. Nearly everyone goes to school, has a job, celebrates birthdays and Christmases, gets married, has children; but the details of your school, job, marriage, are unique. What was the feel of your wedding dress? What did the clock on the mantelpiece look like in your first adult home? What kind of tree was that outside the front door? Who did you meet on your first journey outside Australia? Write your unique details.

Which details?

How do you know which details to include? Random or excessive detail can become tedious. You have probably listened to someone tell you all about their trip to Europe, and despite its being an interesting topic, you quickly become bored. The fact is, our minds cannot absorb too many details: we simply pack up shop at a certain point and stop listening.

It is important, then, to be selective with the details you choose. Include the most memorable, even if they seem unusual or out of place. These mark the uniqueness of your experience. I remember, for example, that when I heard of a dear friend's fatal brain haemorrhage, I first thought, 'Now she won't be able to finish my curtains'. It seems odd, even heartless, that I should have thought such a trivial thing. But this is a real detail of real life, not a sweetened Hollywood version, and including such a detail helps to convey the jerky, searing state of mind that sudden tragedy can cause.

Go back in your mind to the events you want to write about. Spend some time moving about the scene, looking at things and people. Then you will be ready to start writing with well-observed detail.

You are the only one who has lived your life. Despite what we share, despite the apparent ordinariness of all that we have in common, each life is unique and miraculous. Your details are unique. Writing them will reveal the miraculous in the ordinariness of life. You are important, your life is important, and your details are worthy of being recorded.

READING

It Doesn't go on Forever

'Like seeing frogs with holes in them, and worms coming out the holes,' said my father suddenly. Then his eyes looked surprised and hurt that such words had come out of his mouth. He grinned, embarrassed.

Mum and I avoided each other's eyes. We didn't believe we had heard it. Not now, not after all he'd gone through. Dad was an ordinary, honest farmer from the western plains. He wouldn't have said something weird in the middle of a sunny day. Not something dredged out of blackness and slime like a horrible surreal painting. The hurt look on his face disturbed the air, then slid away into the slow minutes of the afternoon.

Dad was never very good with words. In the circumstance it sounds like a bitter joke to say that and perhaps it is. We were sitting under a jacaranda tree. It wasn't in its blue-purple glory but had the green and spreading canopy of late summer. It grew in the grounds of the psychiatric unit at Royal Prince Alfred Hospital, where my father was a patient. Below where we sat we could see the playing fields of Sydney University and hear the cries of healthy young men as they belted their bodies around the oval in training for some achievement or other. From this distance the grass looked perfectly smooth and the figures perfectly formed, like a painting of idyllic youth. Further away, golden light warmed the sandstone buildings of the lecture halls and colleges and they looked permanent and unquestionably worthy.

My father had not been educated past primary school. It was a one-roomed schoolhouse, with rails for tying up horses at the back and a vast pepper tree under which sandwiches and apples were eaten in summer. My brothers and sisters and I went to that same school. By then the hitching rails had fallen down, but the pepper tree still shaded the eating of egg sandwiches and endless red-faced arguments. We all went on to the convent high school in town and then to university, but Dad had left at the end of primary school because his father needed him to help on their farm.

It was the early 1930s and farmers out west still used horses to pull their ploughs and travel about the district. As a teenager, my father sat on the plough guiding the horses as the ground was turned, and then on the combine as the wheat was sown, silent from sun-up to sunset except to yell 'Giddyup there!' or 'Whoa!' I don't know what he thought about all those clear autumn days. He did tell me once that it was beautiful to see the rows straight and fresh as he swung the horses around at each end of the paddock.

But he wasn't alone all the time. On Sunday afternoons other young people rode over on their horses and played tennis. Dad's family wasn't rich, not even well off, but everyone in the country in those days had a tennis court. It was like having a shearing shed, a necessity. Dad must have been quite athletic—he still has a few old tennis trophies at home in the back room.

As he got older he became plump, even though he worked hard in all seasons. He also lost most of his hair, although we rarely saw his head bare. In summer he wore a straw hat for harvesting and in winter a knitted beret-cum-skullcap, which gave him a misleading bohemian appearance. When he went to town he always wore a felt hat of the kind that has become fashionable lately, but he wasn't a smart dresser or a sociable man. He didn't go out except to family weddings or to clearing sales, where he delighted in finding bargains and treasures. Wherever he was, he seemed to sit quietly and watch. He wasn't much of a talker.

I suppose his shyness may have been because of his cleft palate. I didn't even realise he had a disfiguring cleft until I was an adult and even now I rarely see it, but I think it made him shy of girls. Girls liked him anyway. Mum says cheekily that it was his legs she first noticed; he was wearing army shorts the first time she saw him. What I remember are his arms. Summer and winter when I was a child, he wore his sleeves rolled up ready for work. His forearms were brown and strong and utterly reliable, a symbol of all safety for me. The skin now was still brown, but frighteningly soft and loose. Soft, old skin on arms has always made me feel sad and afraid. I didn't want to look at his arms trembling slightly in the patterned light under the jacaranda.

This is from the opening of a story called 'It doesn't go on forever', which I wrote about my father. I have included a piece of my own because it gives you an idea of the kind of life story writing I have done, and because I think it illustrates the use of well-observed detail. Such details as the seasonal stage of the jacaranda tree, my father sitting on the plough, the kinds of hats he wore, the skin on his arms, give a feeling of the emotions I experienced and the kind of life he lived.

WRITING EXERCISES

1 Physical details

Think of someone from your teenage years, a fellow student, a teacher, someone you worked with, whom you remember in connection with a physical characteristic. It may be a turned-up nose, a thick black plait, a tall, skinny frame, a beautiful smile. Starting with that characteristic, write a detailed description of the person. Make it a moving rather than static description, that is, show the person in relation to events rather than in photographic detail.

2 Unique experience

Write as much as you can about something that has happened to you which is unusual or which you believe to be unique. Try to convey the unique flavour of the experience by concentrating on the particular details. Write for 30 minutes.

3 Big event

Write about an important event in your life. It could be a wedding, a birth, a promotion, an award, arrival in Australia, a funeral, an anniversary. Try to focus on the particular details of what happened that day rather than the general outline of the event. Make it your own wedding, not just anyone's wedding.

4 *Appeal to the senses*

Think of a place that has been important to you. It may be a house where you have lived, a cafe you have visited often, a foreign country you have travelled in, a little beach you have sat on. You needn't have stayed long in the place you have chosen to write about, but it must be somewhere that has stayed in your memory as a sensory experience. Try to evoke the sensory detail of the place—the sound and sight and smell and feel of it.

LIFE STORY WRITERS

This short piece, by Katherine P., describes a beach entirely in terms of the senses. Part of her life story was her love of nature. She decided to concentrate entirely on the physical sensations of nature and to use the present tense, which made the writing rich and sensual.

Beach

It is a fine day in winter. To reach the little beach I have first to walk through the old banana plantation. Here there is no horizon, just the rustling of old leaves, and above, a seahawk coasting through pale blue.

Then I enter the dank rainforest with a steep muddy track beneath my feet. Trees claw above and beside me. I bend double to avoid their dampness, imagining leeches already inside my socks, clinging to my legs.

It is dark and it smells. I only want to reach the cold hard rocks at the bottom of the track, to climb over them and jump with relief down onto the warm clean sand.

The beach is tiny, but facing a vision of infinity as the waves merge backwards into the blue, upon blue, upon faded blue.

I sink into the sand and remove my shoes and socks. I stretch my toes to soak in the gentle sunshine and let the breeze run between them.

No leeches to remove today. No warm sticky rivulet of dark-coloured blood. I remove my trousers to be sure. I can relax now, stretch out and feel each limb extending, and dig my heels through the veneer of warmth and into the cool sand.

The following extract, by Bliss, is a description of an important place in her life. In this extract I have not been able to include her whole description of the African village where she and her friends often stayed in the 1930s. Notice how she evokes the atmosphere of the bar. The visual detail reminds one of Rick's bar in *Casablanca*!

The Village

Our place was behind the boatyard servicing the ferries plying between Ada and Keta on the border with French Togoland. Through the gates of the compound we would be greeted by the grinning faces of Tetteh and Mossie. Tetteh, the wrinkled old watchman, slept permanently on the verandah on an old pallet. Mossie was our fifteen-year-old boat boy, who scrubbed down and bailed out our little fleet. If we wanted to sail, then he would rig *Tcheena*, my beloved 14-foot sailing dinghy.

Sometimes when we arrived on Friday night, the drums would be throbbing in the village. 'Who is dead?' John would enquire. 'Father for Yao Kodzo, he go die dis morning. He be small chief and there be wake tonight, Master.' That night sleep would be difficult with the noise of the wake-keeping in the compound of the ferry services next door.

But we knew how to escape the insistent thrumming of the drums and would drive half a mile to Hushie's Bar, clinging precariously to a narrow sand spit, bounded by the ocean on one side and the Volta on the other. Entering the low-ceilinged, dim old bar, smoky with the fumes of generations of kero lamps, we had to duck our heads. The shelves were stocked with meagre provisions, evaporated milk, sardines, tomato paste, bully beef, mosquito coils, candles, and a selection of nails.

Traditionally the bar was the haunt of smugglers who brought alcohol and cigarettes from over the French border. The endless waterways and lagoons which made up the delta made it impossible for police and border guards to control the flow. At the height of the deprivations of life under a dictator, we were not averse to partaking. 'I have the brandy you like,' old man Hushie would whisper. He knew our predilection for Remy Martin. His own idea of a good brandy was Martell. Once upon a time, rumour had it, the Hennessy representative had tried to break into this lucrative market. He visited the border, called together all the smugglers and offered them two cedis a case, the equivalent of a dollar, to smuggle Hennessy instead of Martell. Martell continued to reign supreme.

At Hushie's Bar, we took our drinks out to the side verandah, greeting Madame Dumas, granddaughter of Alexander Dumas of *Three Musketeers* fame. She was a Creole who lived permanently on the compound overlooking the sea.

The roar of the surf prohibited any but the most desultory conversation. The balmy trade winds brushed across our bare arms and thighs while, above, the Southern Cross shone more brightly than in any other sky. Before long, a wonderful doziness would steal over us and we could return to fall flat on our stretcher beds, oblivious to the noise of the funeral drumming alongside.

On Saturday morning in daylight the full glory of the Volta River lay before us. It had wound its way some 70 miles from the dam at Akosombo and by the time it reached our compound had only a few miles left to reach the sea. When the dam was finished in 1965 it covered 3000 square miles and was the biggest man-made stretch of water in the world.

The river was fresh until about ten miles from the sea and a health hazard to all who lived by it. The rapids were home to the mosquitoes which caused river blindness, and then there was bilharzia, which flourished in fresh water. The end result of bilharziasis was blood in the urine, which for many years caused Africans who suffered from it to believe that men also menstruated and that there was something wrong with those who did not, like the cripples who never entered the water.

The steady hum of market affairs rose on the air. A stream of women wound their way to the market place carrying their wares in wok-like containers resting on circular pads perched on their heads. The top halves of their bodies did not move, all walking motion being transferred to their waggling bottoms and the soft flap flap of their thonged or bare feet. No wonder African men find their women's bottoms a sign of beauty.

Small stalls and trestles shaded by banyan or palm trees with shelters of plaited coconut fronds occupied the hard-packed earth alongside the river. The offerings of the day were dried fish, known as stink-fish. Non-African women in the first stages of pregnancy were well advised to avoid the smell. On one table reposed the large 'cutting grass', a creature highly prized and considered to be good bush meat. We had seen this cane rat caught earlier on as he ran out of the tall grass. Another stall had some strange-looking pebbles known as *aggrey* beads, used in tribal ceremonies, and alongside were the aphrodisiac tiger nuts.

Our children's favourite 'fast food', *kelewels*, could be bought from a charcoal brazier at which the mammy offered fried plantain covered with hot pepper sauce on a coconut leaf.

Adinkra cloth hung in serried lengths of 12-metre pieces, beside which were lengths of Kente cloth, each with its characteristic colours, forms and designs. A stole of a certain design given from husband to wife could indicate that he wished to divorce. This happened to me when I received one as a welcome gift on arrival in Africa. *He* had not been told the significance of the design.

Upstream of the market was the jetty where the seagoing trawlers tied up every afternoon, instantly surrounded by a milling crowd of village women, gesticulating, laughing, haranguing each other—the whole gamut of human emotion contained in this microcosm. The fish, distributed in short order, would be displayed on trestles of the Sunday market or already on its way to the city by a mammy wagon adorned with the ubiquitous decal *Whatever you do, six feet under*, to remind us that six feet underground is never far away from any of us.

Turn to the next workshop for discussion and exercises on writing about the important issues of your life.

12
Workshop IX:
Telling your
truth

'Tis strange—but true; for truth is always strange;
Stranger than fiction.

Lord Byron

BIRTH AND DEATH, love, beauty, truth,
fear, passion, grief, joy: these are the 'big issues', experiences that can be overwhelming. They are so 'big' that
it is difficult to know where to start when you want to
write about them.

But it is natural to want to do so. These issues are
the bones of our existence, they lie beneath our daily
life all the time. We could not call ourselves human if
we had not experienced at least some of them. Since
ancient times, in cultures all over the world, these topics
have been written about.

It is difficult to discuss the big issues. The words
themselves—truth, joy, grief—seem to create a kind of
smokescreen between the powerful reality of these experiences and its communication to others. Perhaps that's

the function of the words, not to express the experiences but to protect us from being overwhelmed by them. In any case, the words themselves are abstract and general, like labels on boxes whose individual contents are hidden. The labels make the boxes easy to identify, but the contents are not interesting or engaging until the boxes are opened and each individual piece is taken out.

Many life story writers also want to connect their own small thread to the larger tapestry of life. Some may want to talk about the larger issues of life using their own life as an illustration. Some may want to place their life in political and social contexts. The following suggestions are for those who want to tackle any of the big issues as they write their life story.

Write the particulars

When I think of the birth of my first son, one of the things I remember is that I wore a loose yellow T-shirt which barely reached the horizon of my round belly. Of my second son's birth I often remember the painting, pinned on the wall nearby, of a child dancing under a rainbow. The two births were distinct, their details unique, just as each of the millions of births in the world are distinct and unique.

It is the same for all the common but powerful events and emotions of your life. Just because they are experienced by millions of people does not mean they are not uniquely yours. To write them as uniquely yours, write your own particular details. As I said in Workshop VIII, it is the detail that is unique.

When the feeling or idea that you are writing about is huge and overwhelming, you may look at what you have written and see a string of cliches. It's as if the language centre in our brain gives up in the face of these huge issues, and trots out some tired stock phrases in the hope that we will go away and stop bothering it with these imponderables. Don't give up, but try instead to recall and record the particular details of your grief or joy or truth.

Instead of trying to describe the feelings, write down the things you saw and did and said. These details will convey the powerful experience—it's almost as if they have soaked in the grief or joy and writing about them conveys the emotion. Write about the brooch your wife wore when you first fell in love; write of the metal bed frame you stared at as you battled cancer; write about the crooked teeth of the policeman who announced the accident early one morning. These things convey the lived reality of your own experience.

Look behind the word

Many of you may have tried to tackle the big issues head-on. Often the issues, being big and strong, flatten you and your writing. The result is generalised writing, crammed with abstract words and passages which sound as if they came from a greeting card.

If this has happened to your writing, you may feel my comments are a bit tough. But your experience is valuable and does not deserve to be trivialised by trite language.

It is more effective to sidle up to the big issues, to have a look behind the important word and see that it is actually made up of lots of small moments. Write about these moments rather than about the big, important word. For example, if you want to write about the importance of having direction in life, instead of writing about the idea, write about the instances when you have found, or failed to find, direction in your life.

Step aside from the truth or idea and try to see it in operation. The essence of any deep insight or experience can only really be conveyed through the way it operates in the world. You can write about love and truth until the cows come home and you still will not have communicated anything unless you look behind the words and write about the everyday manifestations of their meaning.

Understate

I saw a documentary on television ten years ago about the postwar soldier settlement scheme. The well-intentioned scheme unfortunately resulted in much poverty and heartbreak. The interviewer asked a woman what it was like on the settlement block in those days of drought and dwindling income. She opened her mouth to speak and then stopped. She was silent for a moment and then a shadowy blind seemed to drop over her eyes and she said, 'It's best not to say, isn't it?' Her telling silence said everything.

Look at that expression 'a telling silence'. It is a contradiction in terms which we all accept because we know that silence can speak. The contradiction contains important advice for writers. It is as true in writing as in conversation that what is *not* said can be as revealing as what *is* said.

I certainly don't mean you should not write about the really important issues of your life. On the contrary,

I think a life story without them would be thin indeed. I do mean that writing is often more powerful when it is understated rather than overstated. A few well-chosen words can be more effective than an outpouring. As William Strunk and E.B. White crisply put it in their useful book, *The Elements of Style* (Macmillan, N.Y., 1979), 'It is seldom advisable to tell all'.

One practical way to understate is to limit your use of adjectives. Remember the exercise in Workshop VI on cutting adjectives. Think of the important topic as a piece of fine porcelain that needs only a few delicate strokes of paint (adjectives) to bring out its essence. Don't pour a tin of paint all over your truths.

Another way to achieve the sharpness of understatement is to limit your use of abstract words. I mean words like beauty, truth, love; words that don't help you hear and smell and touch. Use these words by all means, but treat them as expensive so you don't spread them around too freely. They are perfectly good words, but if they are overused they start losing their force.

Above all, trust that those reading your life will have experienced some of the same emotions. Let them connect to your experience in the silence around your words. In other words, try not to over-explain. Holding back a little will give what you do write more power.

Move from detail to 'big picture'

Many of you may want to write about your life in relation to the larger world. This may involve the political and social environment or it may mean putting your life in a wider philosophical and moral context.

Instead of having separate sections on politics and

social conditions, or on your philosophy, I suggest you weave these into your personal story. Start with a personal detail and use it as a springboard for writing about a connected issue in the wider world. For example, you could write about your brother enlisting for the Second World War and use that as a way in to expressing your thoughts on the morality of war or discussing the social impact of the war on Australia at large.

This idea of moving from the personal detail to the general experience applies to the whole area of writing about beliefs, philosophy, values. Too much abstract philosophical discussion becomes dry and can begin to seem airy and insubstantial, even when it is your life-blood. Most of us need a good solid table of concrete events that we can see and lean on as we discuss philosophy. Give us the table and we will happily listen to your thoughts.

READING

On the Verandah

She [my mother] sometimes helped a woman in labour before the doctor arrived, or a family with influenza in the wet season, or a man who'd spent time in the northern islands and now had a recurrence of dengue fever—fever so bad that his skin had grown horribly sensitive, his headaches were unmanageable, and he had become delirious, raving alone in some small, dirt hut two or three miles from the nearest scrub track. Once I tagged along behind my mother to such a hut where an old man needed help, and found that the walls of rough bush timber were plastered over with pictures cut from magazines: there were beautiful girls in very modest bathing suits and early cars and smart people attending the races. I remember climbing onto a stool to gaze at them. Another time it was a curly-headed Irish girl whom my mother helped. 'God love her,' the girl said about a year after the accident, her eyes uplifted under her bangs. 'It was on the verandah of the dairy cottage on your father's place, and there was a big tub of scalding water, and it was in the dark, and I fell into it. If your mother hadn't known what was best to use, I don't know whether my face'd be here today.'

So life went on in the shadow of the scrub, with the creak of great trees falling, with the monsoon rains fertilising the new grass and corn, with the cows multiplying and their poddies sucking our fingers as we taught them to drink from buckets instead of from their mothers. None of the novels we had read about English life prepared us for what we were actually experiencing—these books which talked about rivalries in Parisian courts; pirates who strung people up and looked for treasures of gold; squires impregnating farm girls without fear of revenge; English villages where manners were restrained, if somewhat waspish; and genteel heroines who waited dutifully to be wooed.

Behind what we read lay the questions of customs and morals, for although Australia had no state church, and in theory gave equal acceptance to all religions, the Anglican Church—to which we as a family belonged—held the dominant role, both numerically and socially (it being, of course, the ruling church of England). At the same time, I think there existed in Australia some sort of natural prejudice against the 'respectable' view. Far away from the mother lode of stern English propriety, there had grown up a desire for less restrictive social rules.

'In Australia,' someone later said to me reprovingly

when I mentioned the convict influence as something which must at least be reckoned with, 'it is believed that human nature should have a second chance.' Implicit in this Australian philosophy was the suggestion that after all it might be better to be descended from a convict or ticket-of-leave man or an impoverished rural immigrant or a lower-class industrial worker than from some effete second son of an old British house, although this notion did not quite jibe with the warm attachment to the 'old country' or with the strong middle-class respectability which many Australians strove for (as if to offset any accusation of coarseness of origin). 'Well,' as my father said, laughing a little, 'we all love England, but even if Englishmen are our brothers they're also bloody pommies.'

This extract is from *A House Among the Trees*, by Joan Colebrook (Chatto & Windus, 1988), which relates her growing up in the 1920s on the Atherton Tableland of northern Queensland. Here she describes the practical details of her family's daily life in relation to their reading and the Anglocentric outlook common in Australia at the time. Her mother and the family are dealing with life in the raw while their minds are being formed by reading books about 'refined' European life.

She moves from the particular details of her family's life and their reading to a general discussion of the differences, then returns to the particular with a comment from her father. This is a technique you can use if you want to place your personal life in a wider social and political context.

WRITING EXERCISES

1 Achievements

Write about your greatest achievement. Its greatness is to be judged by you alone. It can be anything from a sporting achievement to a personal fear overcome that no-one else has ever known about. Remember to give the particular details which make it your individual triumph.

2 Ten words

In one minute, write ten words that apply to you. Do not think about them beforehand and do not cross anything out. When you have finished pick one of the words and write for twenty minutes about yourself in a real situation that illustrates how the word is connected with you. Do not include the word itself anywhere in the piece. You can, of course, do this for every word in the list. You will come up with some good pieces to include in your life story.

3 Evidence

As in Workshop II on sources, take a document from your life: birth certificate, school report, marriage certif-icate. For this exercise, try to connect the document to the bigger issues of your life. Let your mind wander for a while before you start so the connections you make are not forced or awkward. Use it as a starting point for talking about your values, beliefs, philosophy.

4 Arriving

If you have come here from elsewhere, write about your

first impressions of Australia. Go on to compare them with what you see now. If you have always lived here, imagine you have just met someone who has arrived from another country and knows nothing about the last twenty years in Australia. Tell them, in writing, about the significant events and the changes that have taken place. Write what you think is important, what you thought about the events and changes, and about their impact on your life. Set yourself to write for an hour at first and see what you come up with. If you are enjoying it, continue.

LIFE STORY WRITERS

The following piece, by Leslie R., is about his first weeks in Australia after arriving from England. He records the detail of his experience and also expands his view to talk generally about conditions and the way things have changed—always a fascinating exercise!

Sydney, June 1953

I arrived in Sydney to warm, sunny days and cool nights. After a weekend in the men's residential at Strathfield, I moved to our rented house and prepared for the arrival of the family. I started work, catching the bus from North Bondi, a noisy utility version of the familiar double-decker London reds with most of the comforts removed. At Central Station I took the suburban electric train to Meadowbank in an uncomfortable twenty minutes. A dusty maroon colour outside, stone and green within, with leather-covered seats and ever-open doors, it rattled and roared along, making conversation a painful business. On some mornings we raced to Strathfield alongside a giant 4–6–2

Pacific locomotive hauling a long-distance train, and the fascination of the close-up view of the working valve mechanism and connecting rods distracted me from my *Sydney Morning Herald*.

In these noisy morning train conversations I learned quickly, like a child in its early years. I was gently baited but carefully avoided giving any excuse for a 'whingeing Pom' label.

'Did you hear about the Pom who was short two bob for his fare back to England? His Aussie mate said, here's four bob, take another of the bastards with you!' We all laughed.

The factory engineer who related this is the same man who, shortly afterwards, saw me struggling from the station to the factory with two heavy suitcases. I was moving that day to our new house at Woolooware, taking the last minute things to work with me. He came up behind me and took the larger of the cases.

'I don't like to see anyone struggling too hard,' was all he said. He was a tall Chips Rafferty, Crocodile Dundee type, quick to take offence but equally quick to help. He liked his beer and one night in a pub talked too loudly and long of the inadequacies of the works manager. Somebody told on him and he lost his job. Aussie mateship cannot always be relied upon.

There is a sponge-like absorption in those first few months: pubs closing at 6 p.m. and the swill that precedes it; illegal SP betting organised on not-so-secret premises; stories of police aiding and abetting; unsewered housing areas serviced by a nightcart, dry sewerage systems or septic tanks; bull ants and Sydney funnel-web spiders; the near-religious status of Anzac Day, Gallipoli and Legacy; the beginning of the long reign of the Menzies government, smarting at first over its failure to ban the Communist Party and making up for it with a near-hysterical welcome to Queen Elizabeth and Prince Philip on their first visit to Australia; polio as ever-present scourge and a back-of-the-mind worry to my wife, Margaret, and I with our three young children; the last evidence of power shortages with the rostering of districts for blackouts. I had the uneasy feeling we might have come to the wrong place.

But this is a time-capsule view of a country in the middle of a great rate of change. The 1956 Olympics produced the liberalising of the licensing laws and hastened the proliferation of exotic restaurants. Sydney's water supply problems were eliminated by the completion of Warragamba Dam. That great white knight in shining armour, the Snowy Mountains Hydro-Electric Scheme, was completing dams and opening power stations on time or ahead of schedule. The introduction of widespread inoculation with the Salk vaccine reduced the fear of polio to negligible proportions.

I cannot remember that at this time there was much discussion of the public school system. As a matter of economic necessity our children went to Cronulla primary school and did well. I now have in my family two PhDs and a BSc, all of them seeking to keep me in the style to which they think I should be accustomed and providing house room in Melbourne, Coventry and San Francisco whenever I feel like it. Whatever the state of the public education system now, I have no reason to be anything but grateful for the start it gave them.

This extract from a longer piece by Katja G. is a response to the third exercise, using a school report as the document. Both Katja's parents were survivors of concentration camps in the Second World War, and her life story, which she has now finished, explores the emotional burden that the children of such survivors carry unseen.

Souvenirs

While sorting through things, I started looking for keepsakes from my own childhood and was amazed at how few reminders there were. I assured myself that my mania for tidiness would have swept away my kids' old junk too. I could hear myself saying, 'I'm not sentimental. I don't need old stuff. I can't stand mess.'

My joy at noticing the trophies perched on the top shelf, the ones I'd always bitched about having to polish, surprised me. And indeed, I was so glad that something had made me tuck away those first crayon scrawls. It was good that the Mother's Day drawings on butcher's paper and the sticky birthday messages had survived my zeal. The corps de ballet of dusty dolls made me smile, and I thought to myself, 'OK, you can stay, you're not really such health hazards'. I was surprised at my sentimentality, amazed that I'd kept these fragments from my children. I realised I'd kept a multitude more in the stacks of photo albums that gave a potted version of our polyglot history of picnics, parties, our physical prowess, holidays, and our own weird brand of humour. It seemed I wasn't as ruthless as I thought. I was pleased at how rich we were.

I only found a few traces of my own childhood—a handful of old black and white photos. I told myself I simply wasn't attached to things. But something else niggled. 'Be truthful,' I murmured. 'There isn't anything you want to hang on to from way back then.' There is no scruffy doll, no old tennis shoe, nor a yellowing first ballgown that I'd bothered to keep.

And I didn't want to think about why my mother hadn't hung onto some pieces of me. After all, I'm a middle-aged woman and should be well beyond all that. But then one old school report did catch my eye.

Everyone thought it was terribly funny when I showed it to them. *Kathrin is apathetic and somewhat irresponsible*, was the censorious comment. My kids and husband hooted with glee. As I looked at it, the shame of over 30 years ago still washed over me. But then I felt angered and saddened for the kid in the report. How little people had understood. No one had bothered even to get the name right. Katja. No one knew this dark-haired, olive-skinned, shy thing, all shut up tight.

An angry tear slid down my cheek. 'It's not funny,' I croaked. 'I was bloody scared and depressed. And they didn't even get the damn name right.'

I guess it wasn't too fashionable in those years to be a confused migrant kid. You were supposed to be glad, after all. Kids weren't really meant to understand adult trauma and fear. 'Run outside and play,' they'd say, and we'd all pretend we didn't hear our mother weep and our father kick the door. And I supposed it did seem we were just daydreaming at school, when we numbly stared out the window.

I looked at the traces my brood had left and I was glad that their imprint was already so strong, glad I had learned so much that was good from them. My mind wandered onto another tack and it occurred to me that collecting is, in fact, a luxury I took for granted. Looking at those cherished ordinary things that take up space made me understand that my childhood was devoid of unnecessary flotsam. The fear of loss, of having love wrenched away, was part of the gaping hollow left by the war. Our parents feared being sentimental, were afraid of being too attached. They were scared of being loaded down, were afraid to lose everything all over again. Ironically, being free and light was weightier.

I was brought back to the present by the noise of my children outside the window. I realised how far we had all come and how much we had collected. Sad and happy stories were just part of our luggage, part of life's collectables, our souvenirs.

Turn to the final workshop for answers to a variety of questions life story writers ask, and for suggestions on topics to write about when you are stuck.

13
Workshop X: Questions, suggestions, topics

My life, I will not let you go except you bless me, but then I will let you go.

Karen Blixen

THIS WORKSHOP IS a restless one. It is the season of change; the ending of the course and the beginning of your separate journey. It is the time, not for steady work, but for sharing possibilities with each other; for acknowledging what has already been done and discussing plans for the future. Now is the time for questions, suggestions and celebrations.

This is when you bring cakes and champagne to the workshop. We sit back with a glass, or a cup of coffee, and enjoy the beginnings we have made and look forward to their completion. In this workshop, then, there will not be the usual readings and writing exercises, although there will be one last exercise. Instead, I will try to answer some questions that regularly arise, and offer a few suggestions in areas that have not come up in other workshops. The chapter after this workshop will look at what to do with your writing once you have finished.

QUESTIONS

How do I end my life story when it's still going on?

Oh yes, that difficult last chapter! You could write a new last page for your life story every day, but assuming you want to finish it, here are a few suggestions.

How to end can depend on the structure you have chosen. For example, if your structure is chronological, you could end with yourself sitting down to begin writing your life story; or if you are writing it as a journey of discovery, you could end with the most important discoveries of your life. Look to your overall structure and you will find the most appropriate note to end on.

Endings can also depend on beginnings. Read back over your opening chapter and see if there are ways in which you could connect the ending to the beginning and so achieve a sense of cyclical completion. For example, if you began with a humorous anecdote, you may be able to finish with one; if you opened with an image from nature, you may end with a similar image.

The recurring themes of your story can help you find an ending. You can use the ending to make a clear statement about the themes, to sum up the important issues of your life. If you have ever wanted to state your case without interruption and have the final word, here's your chance.

You may like to finish with a glance towards the

future. You have been exploring your past for a long time; a look forward can make a very satisfying ending. You can write about your own future, the future of your family, the future of society.

It can be very interesting to finish by comparing the world at the beginning of your life to the world now—the changes you have seen. This is especially useful if you have been writing about your life as a piece of social history. It is fascinating to see how much the world has changed in one's own lifetime.

How do I write the life story of a family member?

Some of you may not want to write your own life story but that of a family member. Many people who come to the workshops want to write about their parents, especially their mothers. I have not met anyone yet who wanted to write about their children—I think it is possibly the last taboo subject!

Most of the suggestions and exercises I have given could apply to writing about a family member. The ideas on structure, storytelling, bringing things to life with dialogue, attention to detail: all of these apply to writing about others. The main area of difference is in the point of view. You are clearly writing from the outside of the person's life rather than the inside, and cannot have the same access to the inner life, although you can make informed suppositions. You can write in the third person (he, she), excluding yourself altogether, or you can include yourself and write from the first person (I) about the family member. Indeed, when you write about someone else, particularly a parent, you are also writing about yourself to some degree.

Some people have tried writing in the first person as if they were the family member. That is, they write a biography as if it were an autobiography. They 'pretend' they are the person they are writing about. I don't feel comfortable with this method and find it confusing to read. I don't think I would like anyone to write about me as if they were me! Still, that is my idiosyncrasy—feel free to try the method if it appeals.

I suggest that you work through the exercises in the workshops, simply changing the subject from yourself to the family member. Make other modifications where necessary—for example, in a childhood memory exercise, ask your subject to tell you a memory and write it down as well as you can. If your subject is a family member who has died, of course you can rely only on your own memories and those of the rest of the family. Remember that you can use documents and any of the other sources I mentioned in Workshop III.

Isn't writing about myself self-indulgent?

Self-indulgence is one of the sharpest insults that can be flung at a writer. Life story writers especially fear that they may be selfishly indulging their own obsessions. They glance around, hoping no-one will catch them at this self-absorbed activity. But what exactly is self-indulgence in writing?

This question was argued for hours in a university class I attended a few years ago. Self-indulgence was generally taken to mean a writer's absorption in his or her own concerns at the expense of concern both for writing technique and for the reader's sensibility. But in practice, each student had a different definition: what one saw as self-indulgent, another felt was honest and moving.

For me, writing is self-indulgent when writers become so absorbed in their own feelings, such as misery, pride, or fondness, or in their own ideas, that they forget their readers altogether. They also forget the role of language in creating the emotions or ideas on the page and so their writing becomes loose and imprecise. They forget the art of writing.

To avoid self-indulgence, I suggest that if you are writing down emotions or thoughts that are particularly important to you, imagine that you are writing them to a discriminating person you know. Consciously consider how you can best convey the truth of your feelings to that person. This takes you one step out of yourself; you are then not so absorbed that you don't think of how others will receive what you are trying to communicate. In this way you will maintain the integrity of your experience and at the same time be able to communicate it to others.

What if I don't want to be identified?

It may seem contradictory that someone should want to write their life story but not want to be identified. But some people have very good reasons for wanting to conceal their identity. They may want to write about traumas or personal struggles, but not at the cost of hurting or embarrassing their family. Or the legal implications of discussing the material openly may be uncertain.

In either of these cases, you may decide to write under a pseudonym and change the names of others involved. You may also need to alter some details, such as dates, place names, names of organisations and characteristics which could identify a particular person.

This is a delicate area, and one in which you need to be very clear about your motives. Take care that you are not setting out to inflict injury. As the American writer Annie Dillard says, 'Writing is an art, not a martial art'. Once you have decided on the necessity of concealing identity, alter as many identifying details as you can without distorting the essential truth of your story.

What if I could be sued for the things I've written?

It may sound unlikely or extreme, but in fact a number of people have asked me this question. If you are at all concerned about the likelihood of a defamation suit, or about the legality of discussing a court case, do consult a lawyer. Even if you have concealed your identity it is worth checking with a lawyer to make sure. Several writers' organisations have legal advisers who specialise in the law as it affects writers. Once you join the organisation, their advice is available free of charge. Contact writers' organisations or the Arts Law Centre in Appendix B for details.

SUGGESTIONS

Eighty topics

Below is a list of some possible topics within a life story. I have put it in the last workshop because it is more exciting for you to make your own journey than to follow a list of topics that may not be particularly relevant to your life. If everyone followed a list of topics, everyone's life story would end up with pretty much the same shape. This list is not to take the place of your own exploration, but to point you in directions you may not have considered. It is also to jog your memory—if you are stuck and don't know what to write next, consult this list and choose a possible new area.

Genealogy; Parents—their characters, background, meeting, marriage, occupations; Own birth; Earliest memories; Homes; Holidays; Childhood friends; Childhood fears; Starting school; Teachers; Favourite subjects; School friends; Fights; Adventures after school; Nature; The beach; Brothers and sisters; My street; Local area; Shopkeepers; Aunts and uncles; Neighbours; Christmas; Birthdays; Grandparents; High school; Moving house; Boyfriends and girlfriends; Going to the pictures; Outings; Books; Conflict with parents; Youthful plans and dreams; First job; Bosses; Leaving home; the Depression; Going to war; Floods and droughts; Changes of government; Politics; Religion; Falling in love; Overseas travel; Courtship and marriage; Being single in a paired world; Giving birth; Children; Turning points; Achievements; Regrets; Best friends; Career; Death of parent; Values; Divorce; Illness; Memorable people; Absurd events; Humorous events; Daily life; My country of birth; Coming to Australia; First impressions of Australia; Learning English; Radio, songs and serials; Sports; Inventions in my life; Retirement; Unfulfilled ambitions; Things I've always wanted to say; Importance of music; Peaceful moments; Weird experiences; Television; Love of animals; The secrets of a happy life; Family sayings; Favourite family stories; Skeletons in cupboards; Involvement in public life; Enemies; Reunions; Blessings.

Humour

Remember the humour of life. It is easy when you are involved in writing your story to become too earnest about your achievements, beliefs and experiences. Don't forget the absurdity of daily life, the funny events, the entertaining people. I don't mean you should force humour in serious moments, but don't forget that there has been laughter as well.

Photographs and illustrations

Remember the family snapshots. Each time I read an autobiography or life story I look at the photographs first. If there are none I feel a little disappointed. Photographs give us a chance to gaze at the person and wonder what they were really like. Photographs from different stages of life are always interesting, as are photographs of parents and other family members or of the family home. Don't forget to identify all the people in each shot.

Illustrations are also interesting. Line drawings of houses or people can add to the text. If you or someone in your family can draw, your work can add a personal touch, a further record of your history.

Recipes and hints

If cooking has been of particular importance in your family, or even if there are a few favourite family recipes, why not include some in your life story? You could have a special chapter for recipes or you could include a few recipes in a chapter about family life. If you have decided to organise your writing around the various rooms in your house, recipes could go in your 'kitchen' chapter.

Household hints handed down through your family

could also be included. Hints which are no longer needed, such as how to whitewash the fireplace, are interesting as indications of a past way of life.

Including hints and recipes lends a very personal touch to your life story and creates a permanent way for the information to be preserved in your family.

Writing drafts

As I said in Workshop I, you don't have to write your life story perfectly the first time. I suggest that you think in terms of two drafts. The first time you are basically trying to get it down on the page. When you have finished, have a break from it, gain a little distance and detachment, and then rewrite. It can be a good idea to show your first draft to other people, as they may be able to see problems that you cannot. Don't show it to everyone, though, or you will end up like the man in the fable 'The Man, the Boy and the Donkey'—unable to please anyone. Choose the person you show it to carefully; you don't want someone to just nod and say 'It's nice', or to tear it to shreds with unrelenting criticism.

Form a Life Stories writing group

It can be difficult to persevere with your life story when you are writing alone. You may start to lose faith in your writing and in the value of your story. You don't know whether anything you have written is any good, and you ask yourself who would want to read it anyway. If this is happening to you, it is a good idea to find other people who are interested in writing their own life stories and form a workshop group. I am sure you won't have any difficulty in finding at least three or four others. You can do the exercises together and read and comment on each other's work. It is much easier to continue when you have like-minded people to encourage you.

If you or your group want further input with writing comment and criticism, or if you think you would benefit from professional life story workshops, contact The Life Stories Workshop, listed in Appendix B.

ONE LAST EXERCISE

In one hour the ability to write will be taken away from you forever. In that hour you have the chance to write whatever you wish to be recorded about your life. It will be the only written record of your existence in the world. Begin.

PART III
AFTER YOU HAVE FINISHED

14
Out into the
world

Writing a book is like rearing children—willpower has very little to do with it . . . You do
it out of love. Willpower is a weak idea; love is
strong.

Annie Dillard

THERE IS NOTHING quite like the mixture
of emotions you experience when you have finished your
life story. There is a sense of pride in your achievement,
joy and wonder at what you have done, and a strange
feeling of loss because it is over. It's as if the retelling of
your life has become as real and important as what is
happening to you now. You have caught the writing
bug and you may never get over it!

Still, you have not finished with your life story yet.
The writing may be finished, the editing completed, but
what do you do with the manuscript? It's a little like
giving birth—the dramatic and difficult work of labour
is over, but now there are lots of details to attend to for

the future. In this chapter I will suggest a few possibilities for your manuscript.

Hand-written manuscript

A hand-written and individually bound manuscript can be a beautiful way to preserve your life story. Mae, a member of one of my workshops, decided that she wanted her descendants to read her story in her own hand. She felt that part of herself was conveyed in her handwriting and that it created an individuality and warmth lost in typefaces. She enjoyed drawing so she also illustrated her story with sketches from her life as well as patterned designs around chapter headings.

This style of presentation is reminiscent of the journals kept by the early women settlers in Australia. For me, there is a certain pleasure in reading these hand-written documents from the past and knowing that the writer's hand pressed warmly on the very page in front of me. With a hand-written life story you can create your own personal historical document for future generations to pore over.

If you choose this option, you will need to decide how you will preserve and protect the manuscript. The simplest solution is to write your final draft into a sturdily bound notebook. Good quality, inexpensive notebooks are available at newsagents or office suppliers.

Another solution is to approach a book-binder—they still exist—and ask for your manuscript to be individually bound and covered. Be sure to consult the book-binder before you write your final draft, as you will need to ask how wide a margin to leave for the binding and what quality of paper to use. Remember, you can photocopy the pages if you want more than the one copy. Having a beautiful and durable document which will become part of your family's history is well worth the cost of binding.

Do not forget to include photographs and illustrations in your hand-written life story. Most photographers can make copies of old photographs, even when you don't have the negatives, so that you can put copies in your book while preserving the originals in an album. Clearly identified photographs or drawings are important to any life story.

Family-sized print run

If you want to give copies of your book to family and friends but do not want to publish for the mass market, you can pay for a small number of copies of your book to be printed. There are publishers who will produce, print and bind your life story for a fee per book. A print run of as few as 50 copies is possible. The fee is less if you can do part of the production yourself. If you have a word processor, and especially if you have a desktop publishing program, you may find this quite feasible. The publisher's fee generally covers layout, book design, printing, binding, and cover design and production. See Appendix B if you want to contact one of these publishers. If you want to distribute your book more widely than among your family and friends, there are a number of distribution networks which individuals can use. Again, see Appendix B.

Getting published

Autobiographies are very popular in Australia. We appear

to have an insatiable appetite for finding out about other people's lives. Albert Facey's life story, *A Fortunate Life,* has been one of the biggest sellers in Australian publishing history. If you feel your life story has something to offer the wider community, you may consider sending your book out to a publisher. First, a cautionary word. There are many people who have written their life story and want to have it published. Of the hundreds of life story manuscripts arriving on publishers' desks each year, only a small number can be published. Don't be too disappointed if you cannot find a publisher. It may be no reflection on your story's value: perhaps the publisher has recently published another similar life story. You can always pay for a small print run as I have described above if you really want to see your story in book form.

When you are deciding whether to try for publication, consider your life story from an outsider's point of view. The publisher is looking for a life story which is well written and which is also exciting, insightful, moving, funny, or different in some way. A story dealing with an area of particular interest such as Aboriginality, adoption, a social or health issue, or an unusual occupation, may also catch the publisher's interest. If your book has something special to say, then it is certainly worth trying to find a publisher.

There are a few details to attend to in the presentation of your manuscript:

1 Send two or three chapters and an outline first. Covering letters must be brief. If the publishers are interested, they will ask for more.
2 Type the manuscript, double-spaced, on A4 paper.

3 Make sure the pages are numbered and identified.
4 The manuscript should not be bound but held together by a spring-backed folder or bulldog clip.

Remember, whatever the reply from the publisher, you have made a wonderful and impressive achievement in writing your life story. That achievement cannot be taken away from you.

THE LAST WORD—EVERYONE CAN WRITE THEIR LIFE STORY

I have on my desk a life story journal which is almost empty. There are only eight pages written on, with barely a paragraph on each page. It was written by Dolly, a friend of mine.

Dolly was a very intelligent, humorous and attractive woman. She was a designer, a wife, and the mother of a sweet two-year-old boy. One day on her way out to lunch with friends, she had a massive cerebral haemorrhage. The next moment, and for the next thirteen months, she could not walk, talk, eat, control any of her bodily functions, laugh, cuddle her son, or do anything except slowly move one hand.

She was cared for day and night, first by the hospital staff and then by the incredible love and hard work of her husband. I decided to try and find a way of working with her to record her life story. I thought it might help her to start piecing her life together again, but mostly it was for me—I longed to communicate with her again.

Dolly began spelling out her story, slowly, so slowly, by dragging her arm across an alphabet board, pointing to each letter, which I then wrote in her journal. It took her minutes to write each word, an hour to spell out a paragraph. I have never seen such determination.

One day in late June 1992 she wrote about her mother, who had died three years previously:

My mother's name was Margaret. She looked like me. She was a smart dresser and very forthright and very honest. I often think of her and miss her. She didn't work outside our home but I think she would have liked to do something—music, I think, because she played the piano. I think she was like me in her personality and in her abilities. She could be very opinionated—about everything. I love her.

When Dolly spelled out the last sentence, 'I love her', I remarked that she had changed tense, and said the present tense made it sound as if her mother were still alive. I suggested that since her mother was dead, perhaps I should change it to the past. Dolly pointed to 'No' on the alphabet board. I suddenly thought, Dolly intends to join her mother.

That was the last time I worked with Dolly on her life story. She died early in July.

Dolly wrote under conditions more difficult than most of us can even imagine. She could only gaze with her large eyes, smile with an awkward movement that looked more like a grimace, and move one hand. Her extraordinary courage and determination have given me the belief that anyone can write their life story. Quite simply, once you decide to write your life story, there is really nothing that can stop you.

Appendix A:
A reading list

THERE ARE WONDERFUL autobiographies or life stories available from all over the world, but because it is impossible to include them all, I have decided to include on this list only a selection of Australian and New Zealand books. If you want to read more widely, *The Bloomsbury Good Reading Guide to Biography and Autobiography* (in the short list of other reading) is a good starting point, although it mainly lists the autobiographies of famous people. This reading list includes both well-known writers and writers who have written only their life story. The books' literary quality varies but they are all valuable life stories. In selecting these titles, I have tried to include writers from as many different backgrounds as possible. I have listed them alphabetically according to book title rather than author because I have found many people remember titles before authors.

AUTOBIOGRAPHIES

A Fence Around the Cuckoo, Ruth Park, Viking Penguin, Melbourne, 1992

A Fortunate Life, Albert Facey, Penguin, Fremantle Arts Centre Press, 1981

A House Among the Trees, Joan Colebrook, Chatto & Windus, London, 1988

A Question of Identity, Ferg McKinnon, Allen & Unwin, Sydney, 1992

As the Catalina Flies, Anna Phillips, Butterfly Books, Springwood, 1993

Childhood at Brindabella, Miles Franklin, Angus & Robertson, Sydney, 1963

Day of My Delight, Martin Boyd, Lansdowne, Melbourne, 1965

12 Edmondstone Street, David Malouf, Chatto & Windus, London, 1985

The Education of Young Donald, Donald Horne, Penguin, Melbourne, 1967

Fishing in the Styx, Ruth Park, Viking Penguin, Melbourne, 1993

Flaws in the Glass, Patrick White, Jonathan Cape, London, 1981

From Strength to Strength, Sara Henderson, Pan Macmillan, Sydney, 1992.

I Can Jump Puddles, Alan Marshall, Longman Cheshire, Melbourne, 1955

Inside Outside, Andrew Riemer, Collins, Sydney, 1992

Letters and Journals, Katherine Mansfield, Penguin, Melbourne, 1977

The Letters of Rachel Henning, ed. D. Adams, Penguin, Melbourne, 1969

Living Black, Kevin Gilbert, Penguin, Melbourne, 1977

Looking for Lisa, Libby Harkness, Random House, Sydney, 1991

Memoirs of a Peon, Frank Sargeson, Heinemann, Auckland, 1974

Moon and Rainbow: The Autobiography of an Aboriginal, Dick Roughsey, Reed Books, Sydney, 1971

My Place, Sally Morgan, Fremantle Arts Centre Press, Fremantle, 1987

No Place for a Woman, Mayse Young and Gabrielle Dalton, Pan, Sydney, 1991

Notes on My Madness, Shirley Lewis, Butterfly Books, Springwood, 1990

Over the Next Hill, Harold Dickinson, Boolarong Publishing, Brisbane, 1982

Poppy, Drusilla Modjeska, McPhee Gribble, Melbourne, 1990

Rachel Weeping, Winsome Smith, Bells Line Books, Kurrajong, 1991

The Road from Coorain, Jill Ker Conway, Alfred A. Knopf, New York, 1989

Ruby Don't Take Your Love to Town, Ruby Langford, Penguin, Melbourne, 1988

Stories from Suburban Road, T.A.G. Hungerford, Fremantle Arts Centre Press, Fremantle, 1983

To the Is-land/An Angel at My Table/Envoy from Mirror City, Janet Frame, Hutchinson, New Zealand, 1984

The Trees were Green, Mary Drake, Hale. & Iremonger, Sydney, 1984

Tracks, Robyn Davidson, Cape, London, 1980

Unreliable Memoirs, Clive James, Jonathan Cape, London, 1980

The Water Lily Man, Kate Llewellyn, Hudson, Melbourne, 1987

Watcher on the Cast-Iron Balcony/Paper Chase, Hal Porter, Faber, London, 1986

The Winter Sparrows, Mary Rose Liverani, Thomas Nelson, Sydney, 1975

OTHER READING

Australian Autobiography, eds J. & D. Colmer, Penguin, Melbourne, 1987

Bloomsbury Good Reading Guide to Biography and Autobiography, eds Valerie & Kenneth McLeish, Bloomsbury, London, 1991

Inventing the Truth: The Art and Craft of Memoir, ed. W. Zinsser, Houghton Mifflin, Boston, 1987

Lookin' for Your Mob: A Guide to Tracing Aboriginal Family Trees, D. Smith and B. Halstead, Aboriginal Studies Press, Canberra, 1990

The Elements of Style, W. Strunk and E.B. White, Macmillan, New York, 1979

Writing Down the Bones, Natalie Goldberg, Shambhala Press, Boston, 1986

Appendix B:
Useful addresses

Adoption queries

Check your local telephone book for the address and telephone number of the government department in your state responsible for community and family welfare. The names of the appropriate departments for each state are:

ACT: Welfare Branch, Housing and Community Services

NSW: Family Information Service, Department of Community Services

NT: Adoption and Social Care Unit, Health and Community Services

Qld: Adoption Registration and Matching Branch, Department of Family Services

SA: Family Information Service, Department of Community Welfare

Tas.: Adoption Information Service, Department of Community Welfare

Vic.: Adoption Information Service, Department of Community Welfare

WA: Adoptions, Department of Community Services
NZ: Adoption Information Office, Department of Social
Welfare

There are a number of other private and religious
agencies you can try. These are listed in leaflets obtain-
able from any of the above state departments. Some of
these agencies offer counselling as well as information.
A good starting point is:

The Post Adoption Resource Centre
171 Glenmore Road
Paddington NSW 2021
Tel. 02 361 0033 or 008 02 4256

Aboriginal identity
NSW/ACT
Link-Up Aboriginal Corp.
5 Wallis St
Lawson 2783
Tel. 047 59 1911

Queensland
Link-Up Aboriginal Corp.
8 Gillingham Street
Buranda 4101
Tel. 07 891 2554

Victoria
Victorian Aboriginal Child Care Agency
4 Brunswick Place
Fitzroy 3065
Tel. 03 419 7899

Northern Territory
Central Australian Aboriginal Child Care Agency
9 Park Crescent
Alice Springs 0871
Tel. 089 53 4895

Karu—Aboriginal & Islander Child Care Agency
PO Box 40639
Casuarina 0811
Tel. 089 22 7171

Western Australia
Yorganop Aboriginal Child Care Agency
Unit 44a Piccadilly Square
cnr Nash & Short Sts
Perth 6000
Tel. 09 227 9022

Bookbinders

Look in the Yellow Pages of your local or state capital telephone directory.

Births, Deaths and Marriages

Check your state capital telephone book for the address of your state's registry of Births, Deaths and Marriages.

Copyright questions

Australian Copyright Council
245 Chalmers Street
Redfern 2061
Tel. 02 318 1788

Distribution

Bells Line Books
PO Box 56
Kurrajong Heights 2758

Genealogy

Society of Australian Genealogists
120 Kent Street
Sydney 2000
Tel. 02 247 3953

Genealogy Research Centre
52 Carrick Way
Torquay 4655
Tel. 071 28 4458

There are also research facilities available at:
NSW State Library
Macquarie Street
Sydney 2000
Tel. 02 230 1414

Illustrators

Rockley Studio
c/- P.O. Rockley
Rockley 2795
Tel. 063 37 9276

Legal queries

Arts Law Centre of Australia
The Gunnery
43 Cowpers Wharf Road
Woolloomooloo 2011
Tel. 02 356 2566 or 008 22 1457

Publishers' addresses

Writers' and Photographers' Marketing Guide
Box 28, PO Collins St
Melbourne 3001

Self publishing

Fast Books
16 Darghan Street
Glebe 2037
Tel. 02 692 0166

Writing workshops, correspondence courses, editing, critical advice

The author of *Writing Your Life* may be contacted through:
Life Stories Workshop
PO Box 4
Hazelbrook 2779

Writers' organisations

Australian Society of Authors
PO Box 1566
Strawberry Hills 2021
Tel. 02 318 0877

Fellowship of Australian Writers Head Office
1/317 Barkers Road
Kew 3101

INDEX

INDEX